COLOR AND CREATE ™

Geometric Shapes and Patterns Coloring Book, Vol.1

Connect with us online to
- Share your colorings with other coloring enthusiasts
- Get free downloads of some of our designs
- Find out about our up-and-coming books
- Get discounts and enter competitions

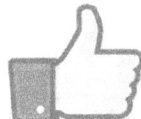

Our Facebook page:
www.facebook.com/colorandcreate

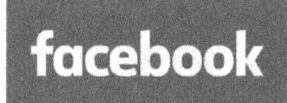

Our Facebook group:
www.facebook.com/groups/colorandcreate

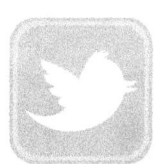

On Twitter:
www.twitter.com/CCColoringBooks

On Pinterest:
www.pinterest.com/colorandcreate

Color Test Page

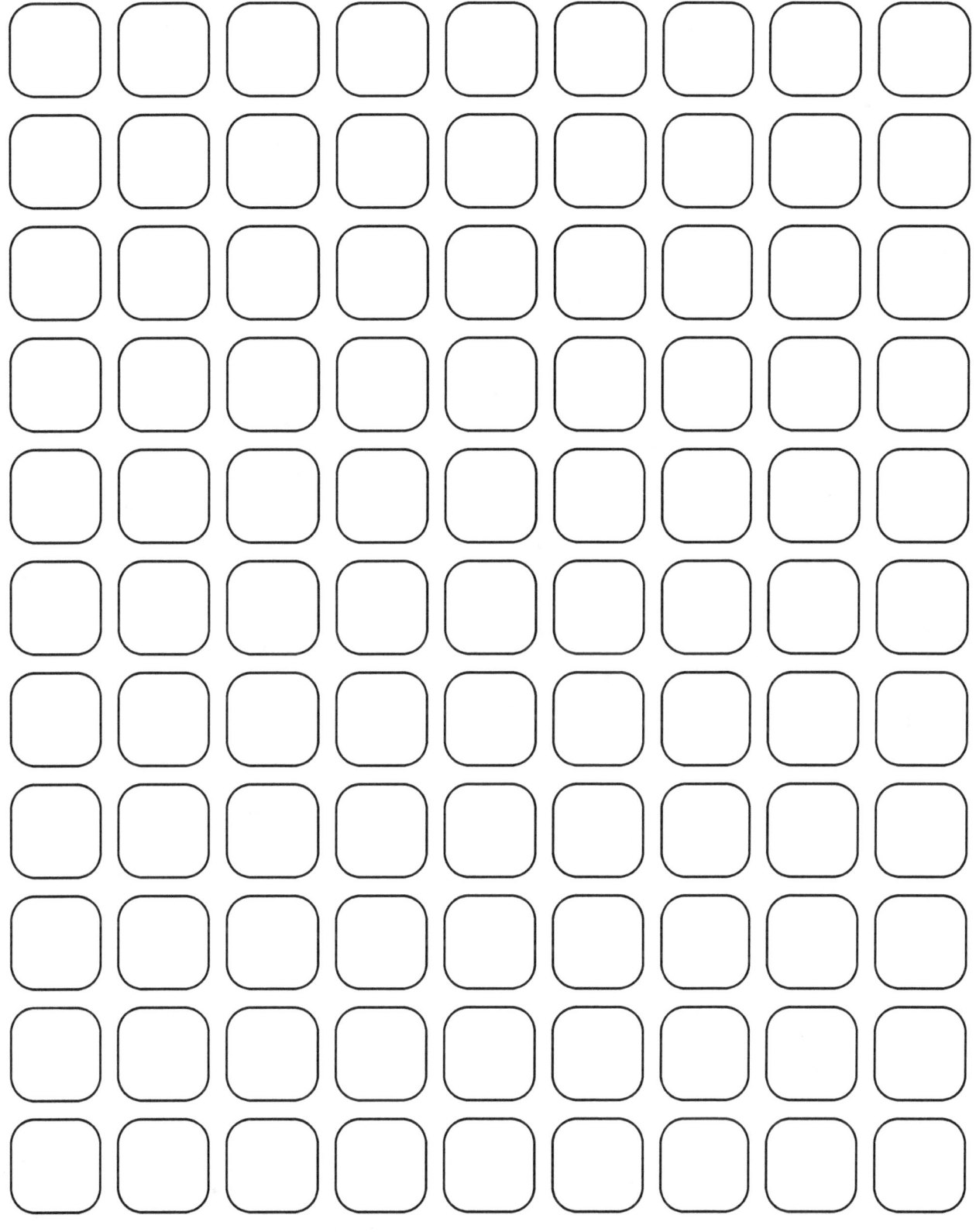

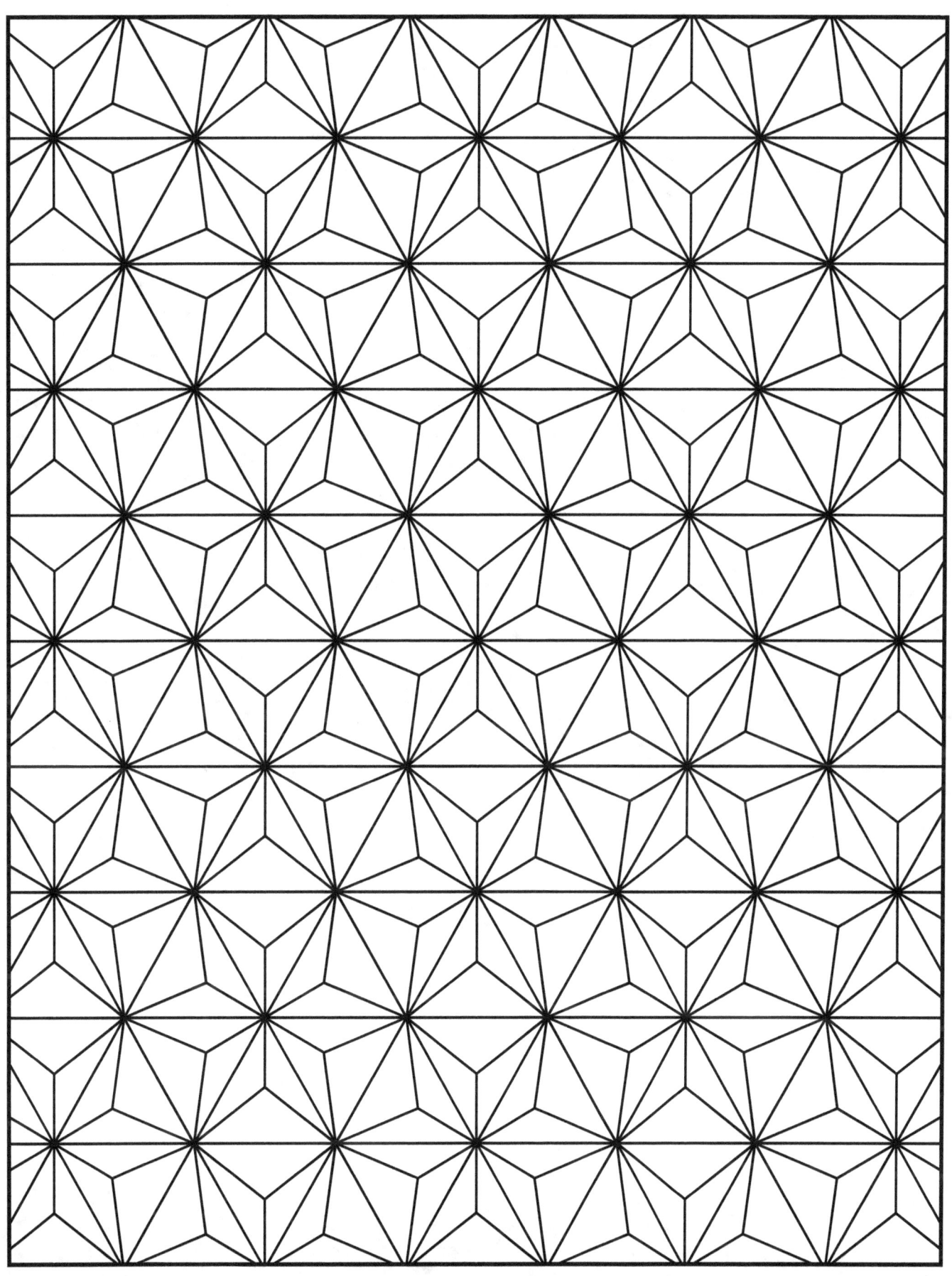

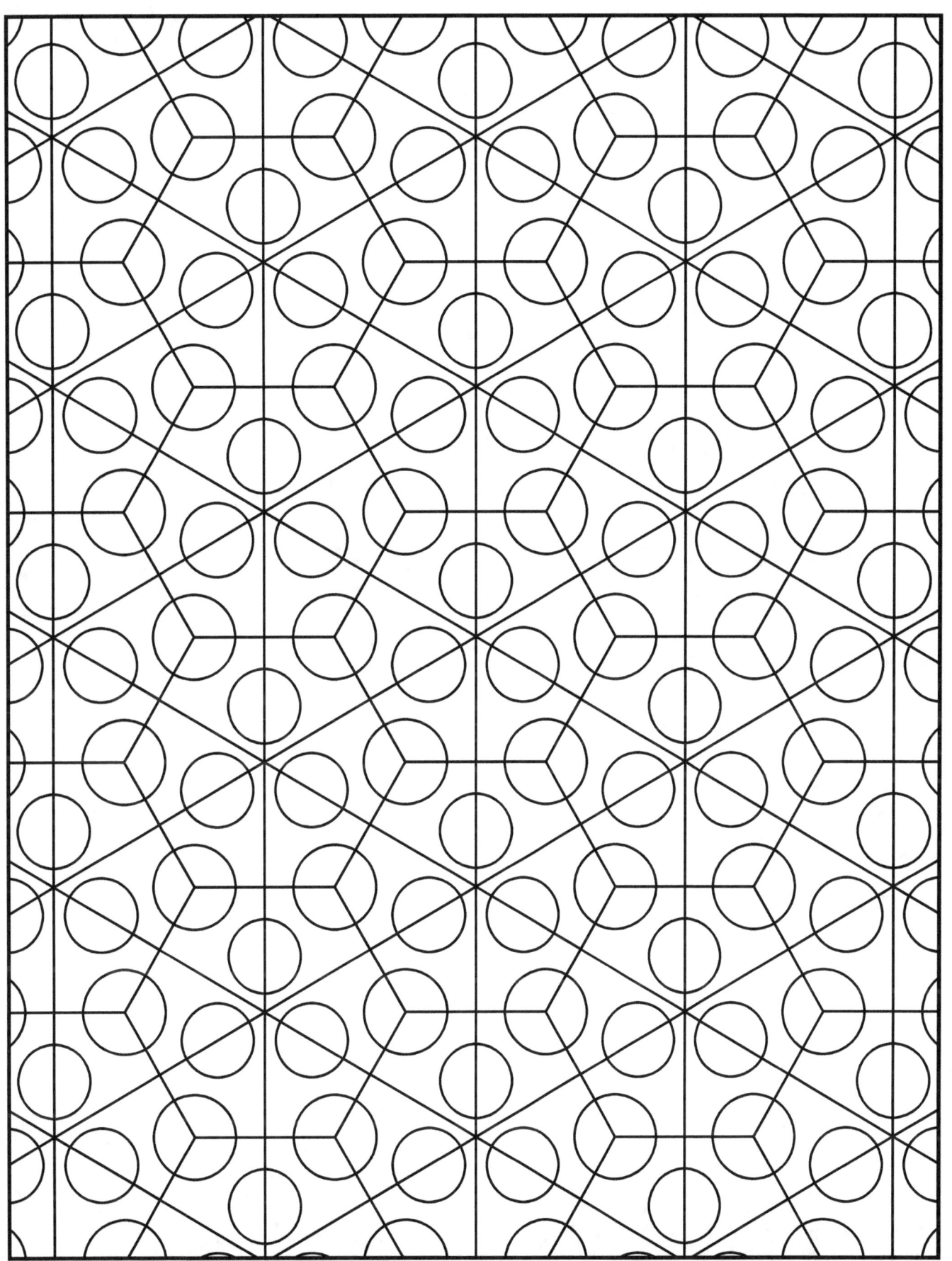

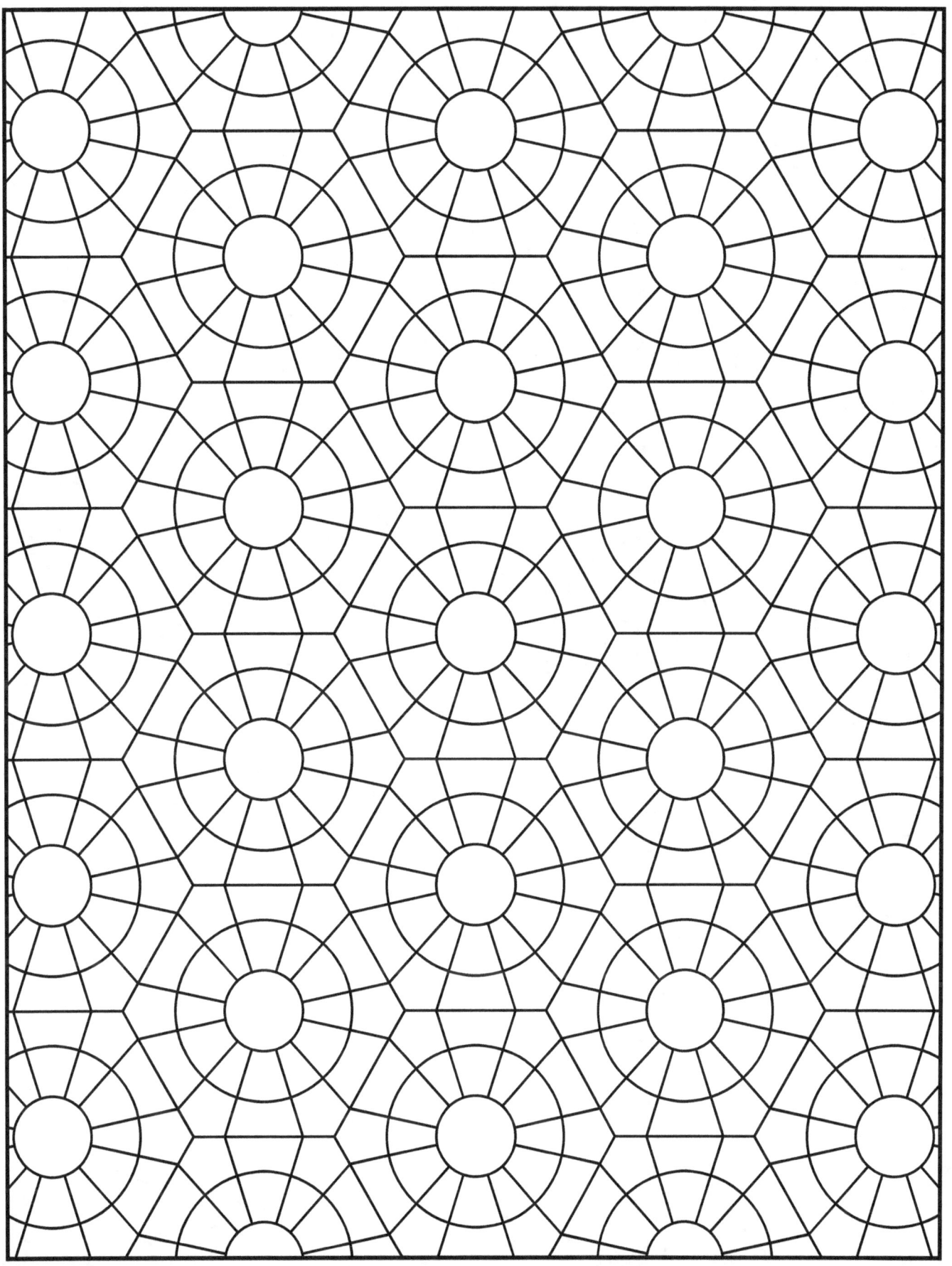

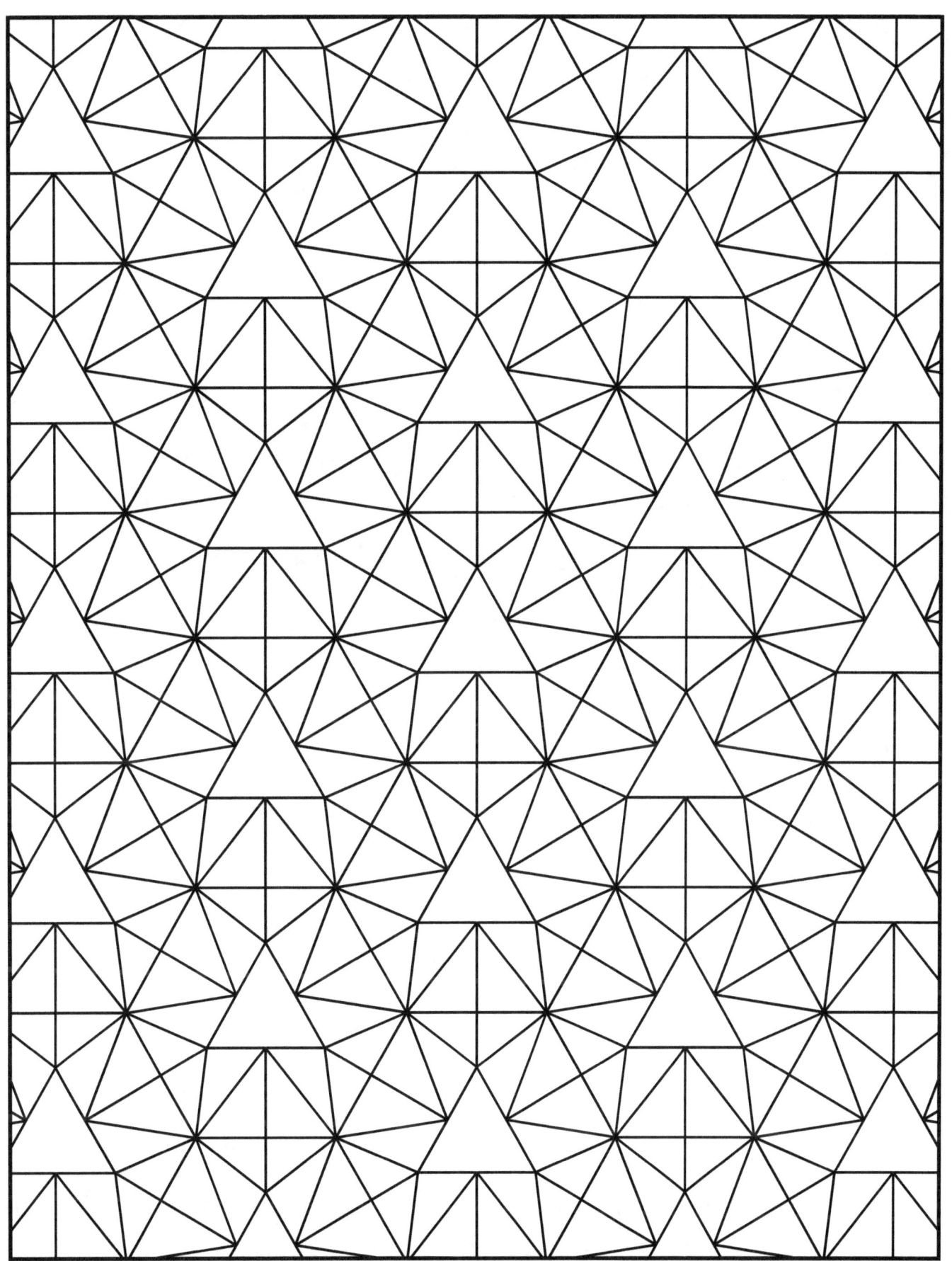

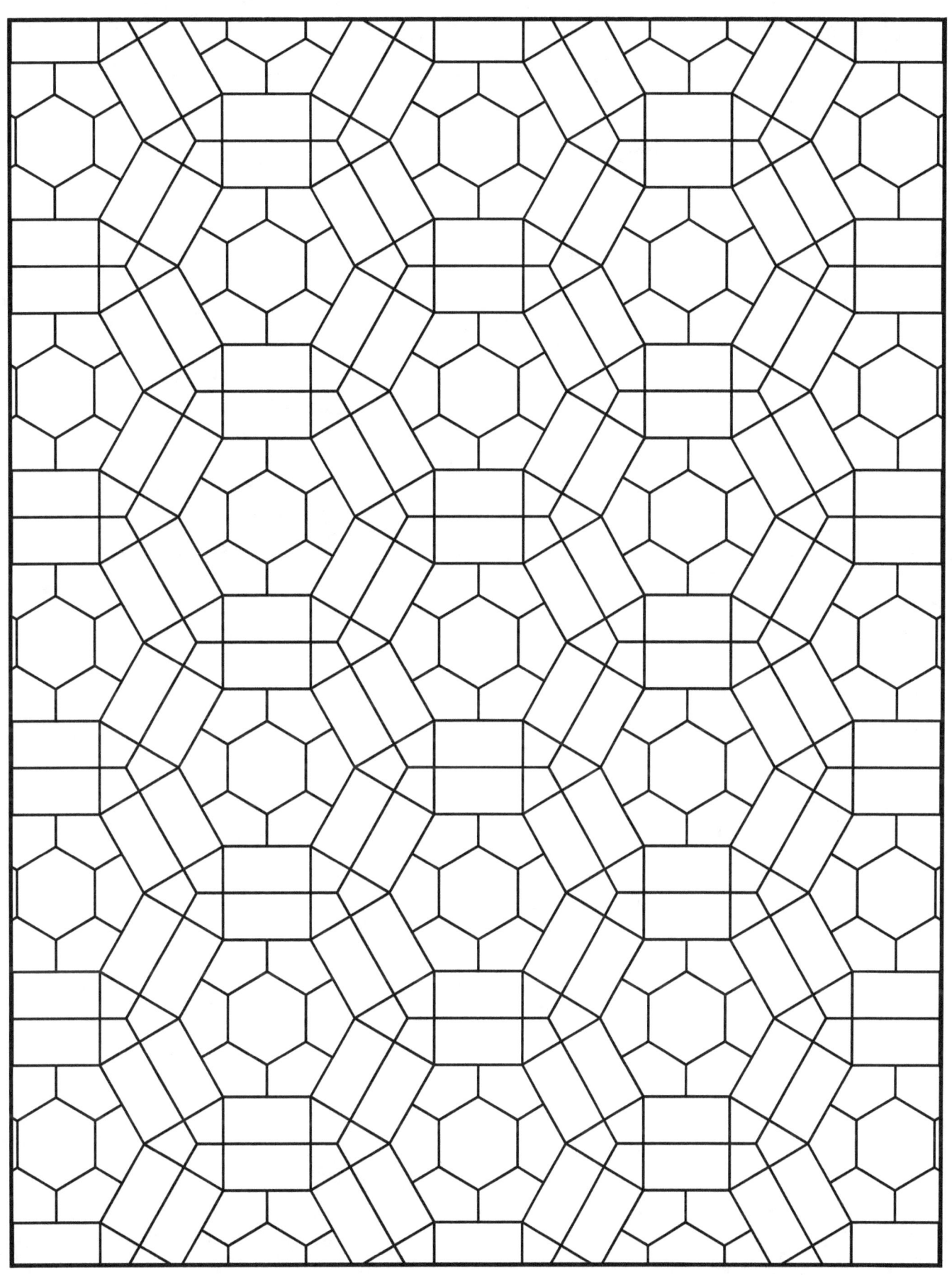

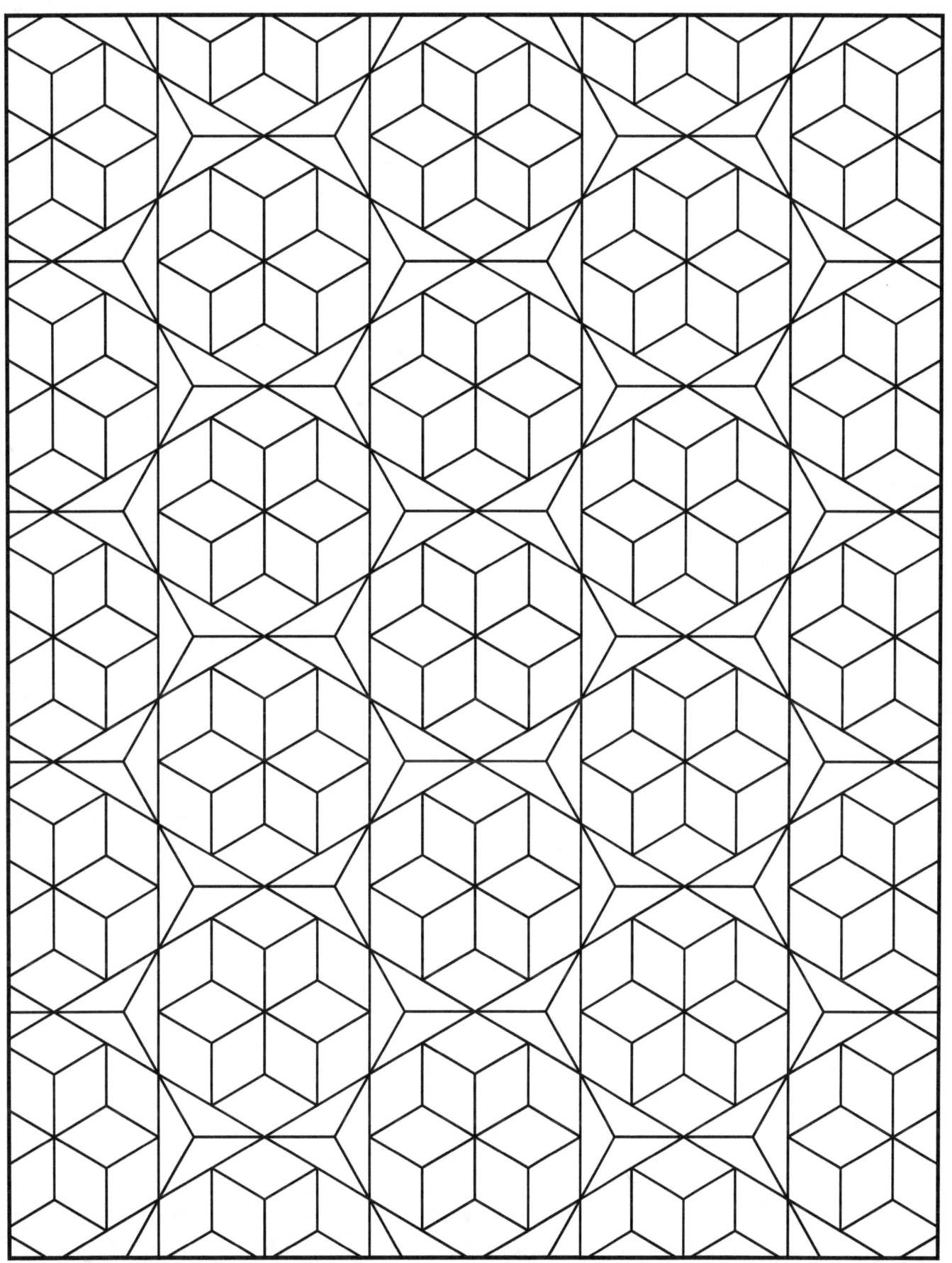

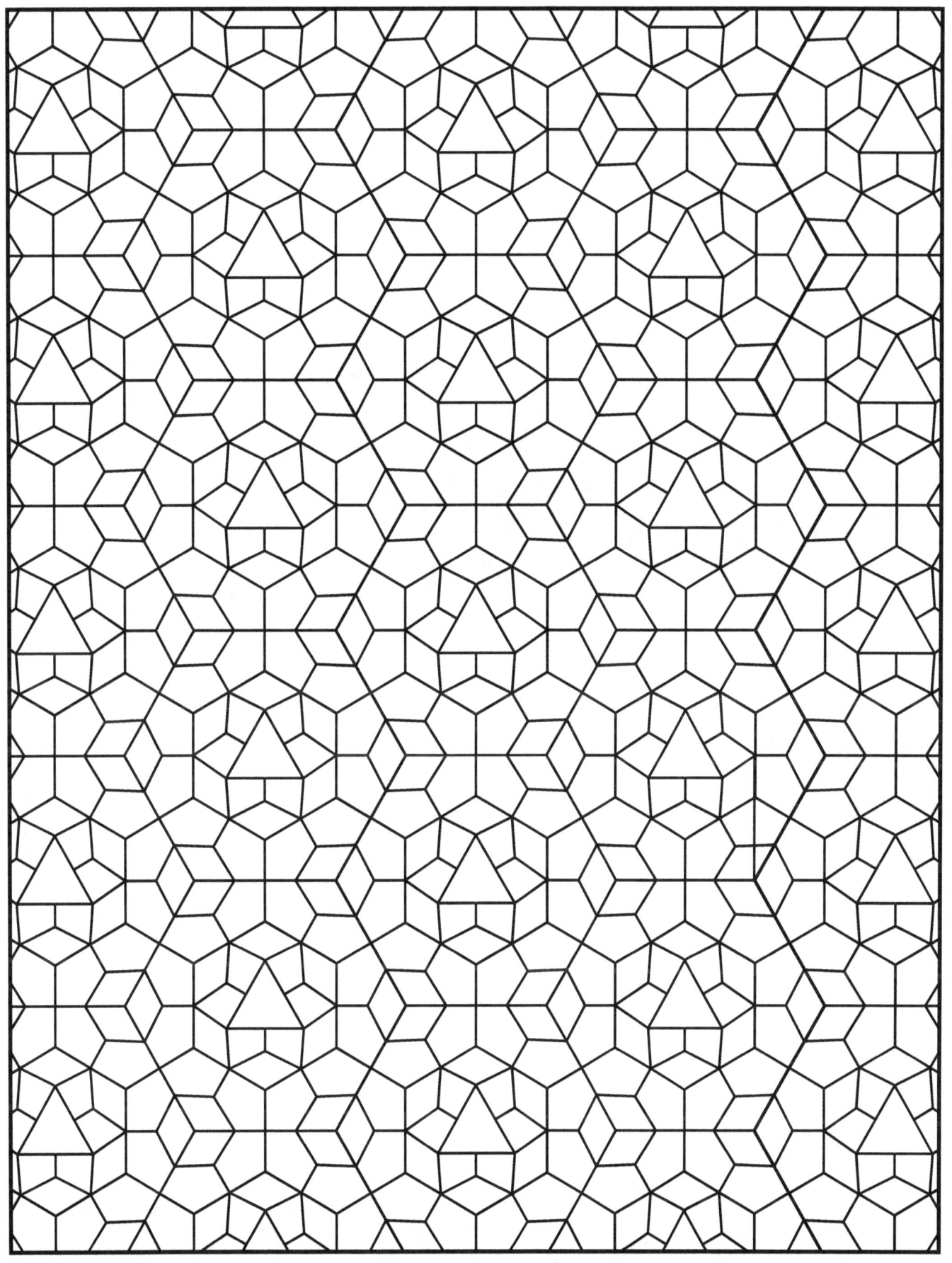

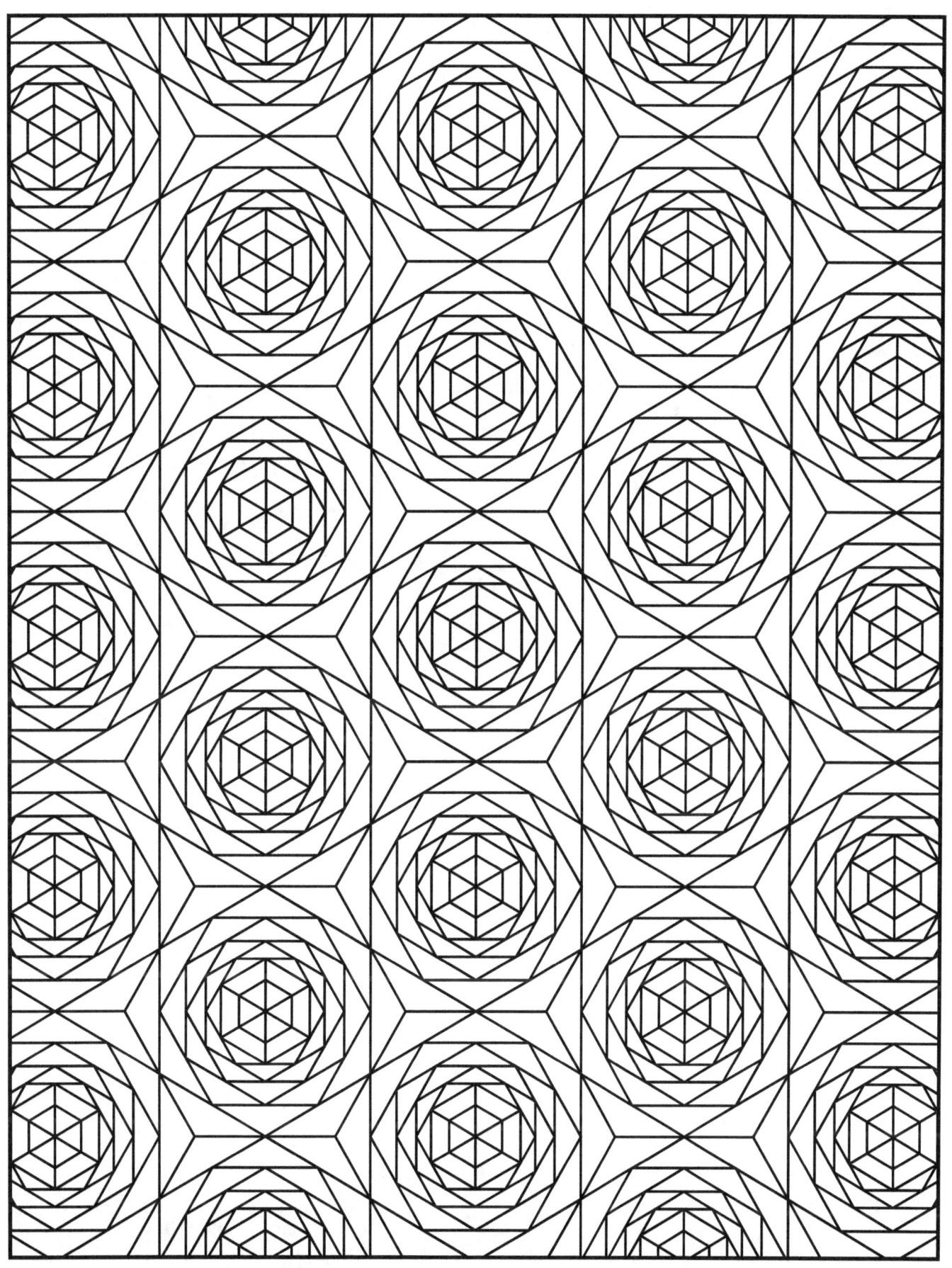

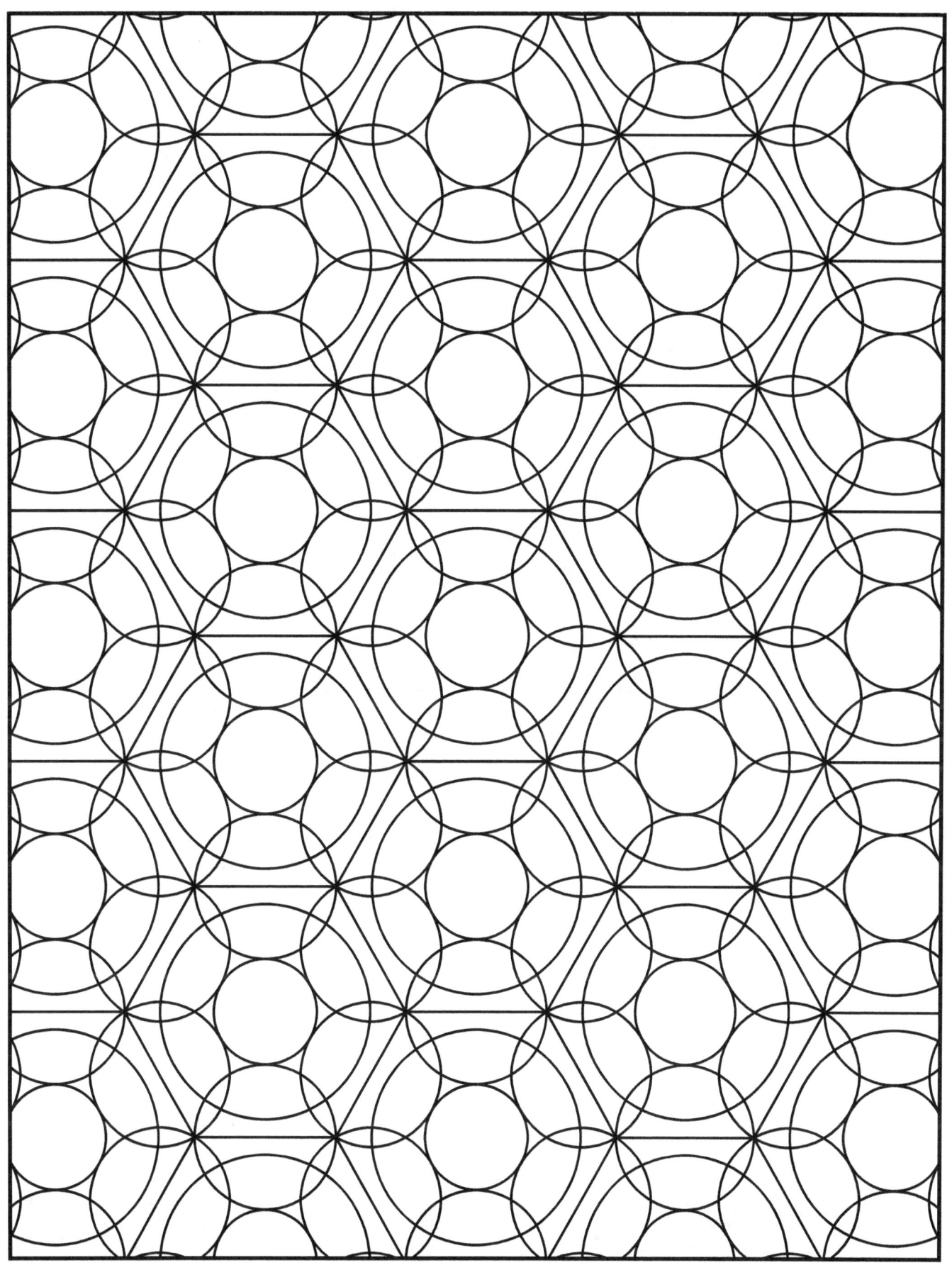

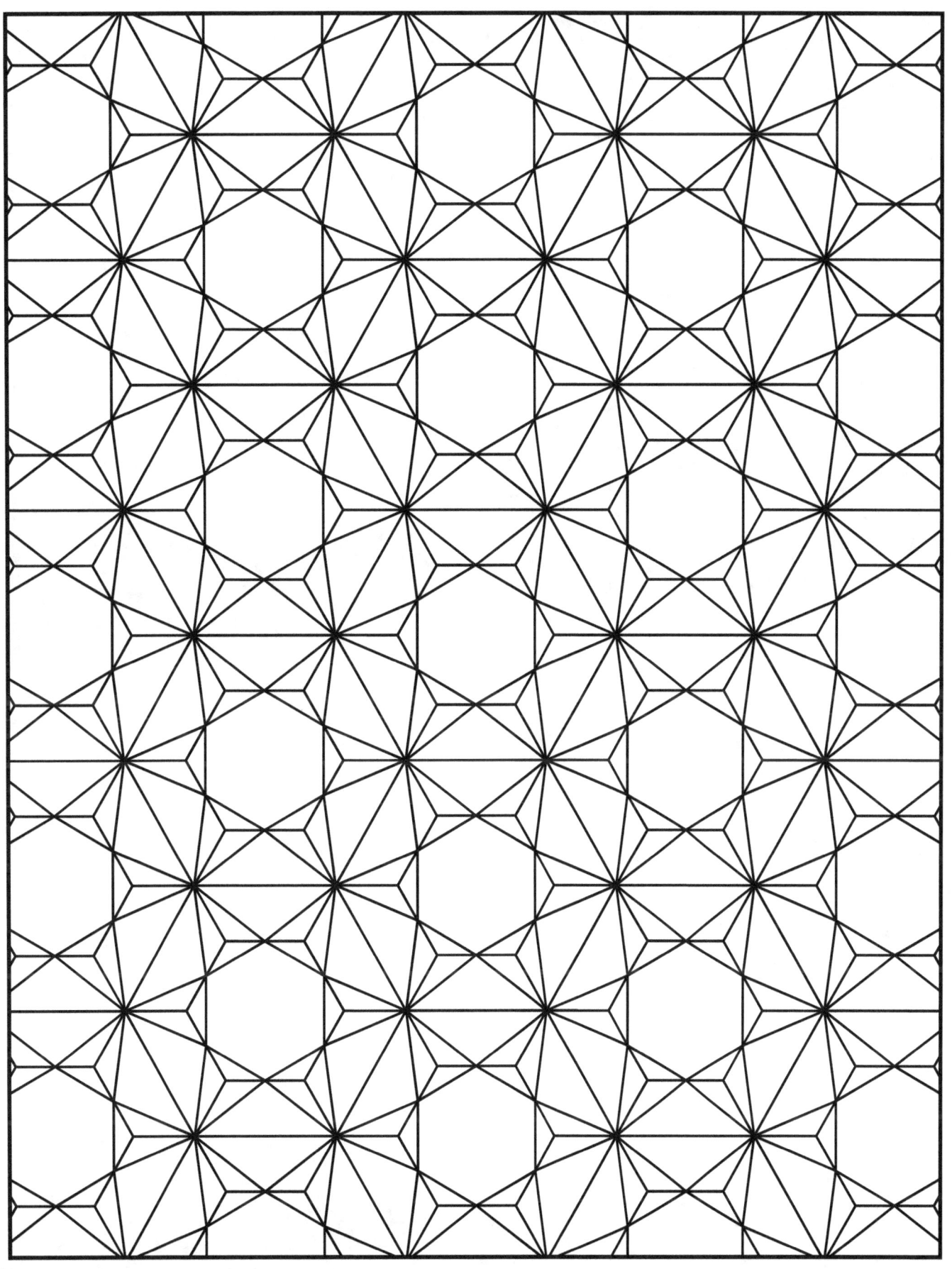

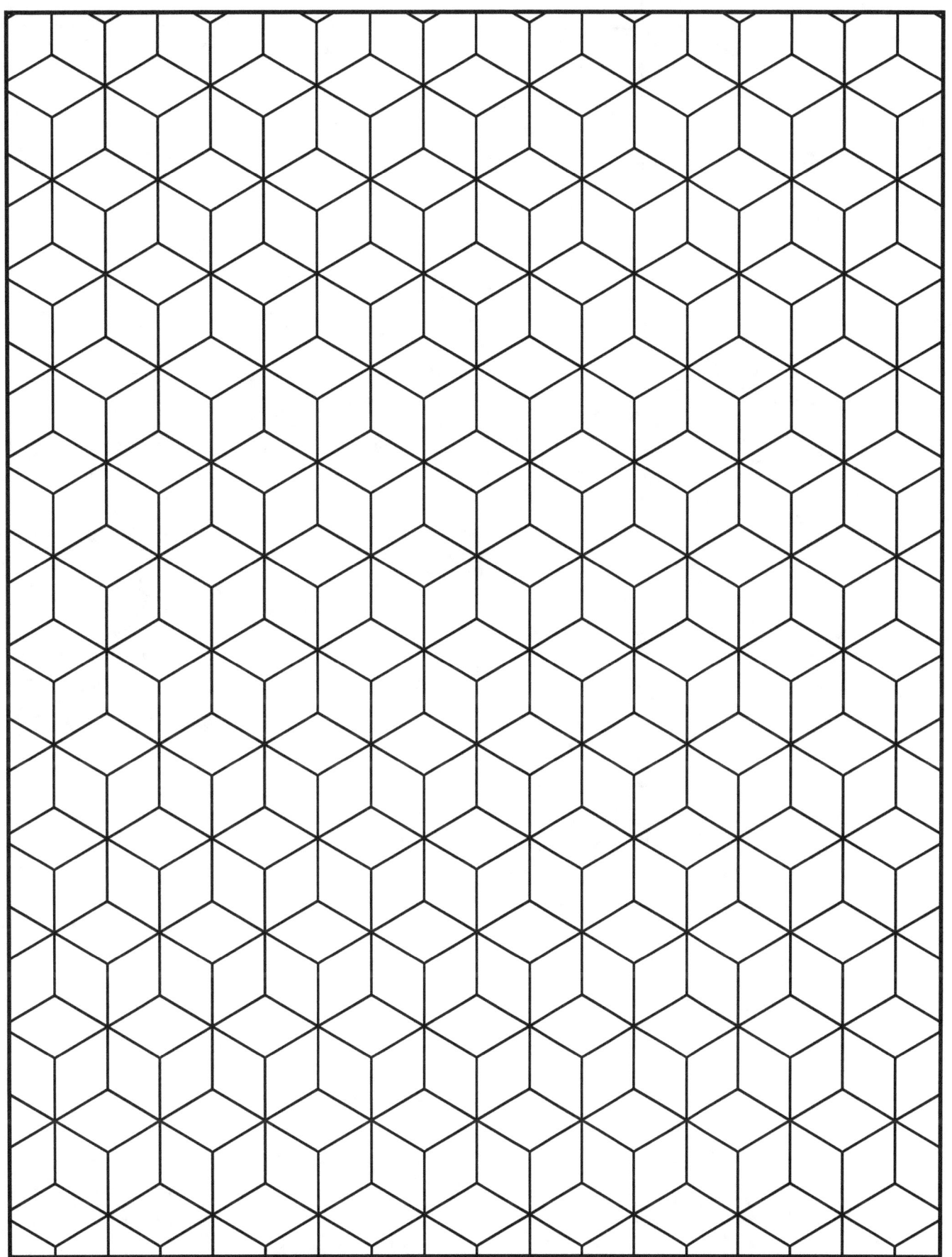

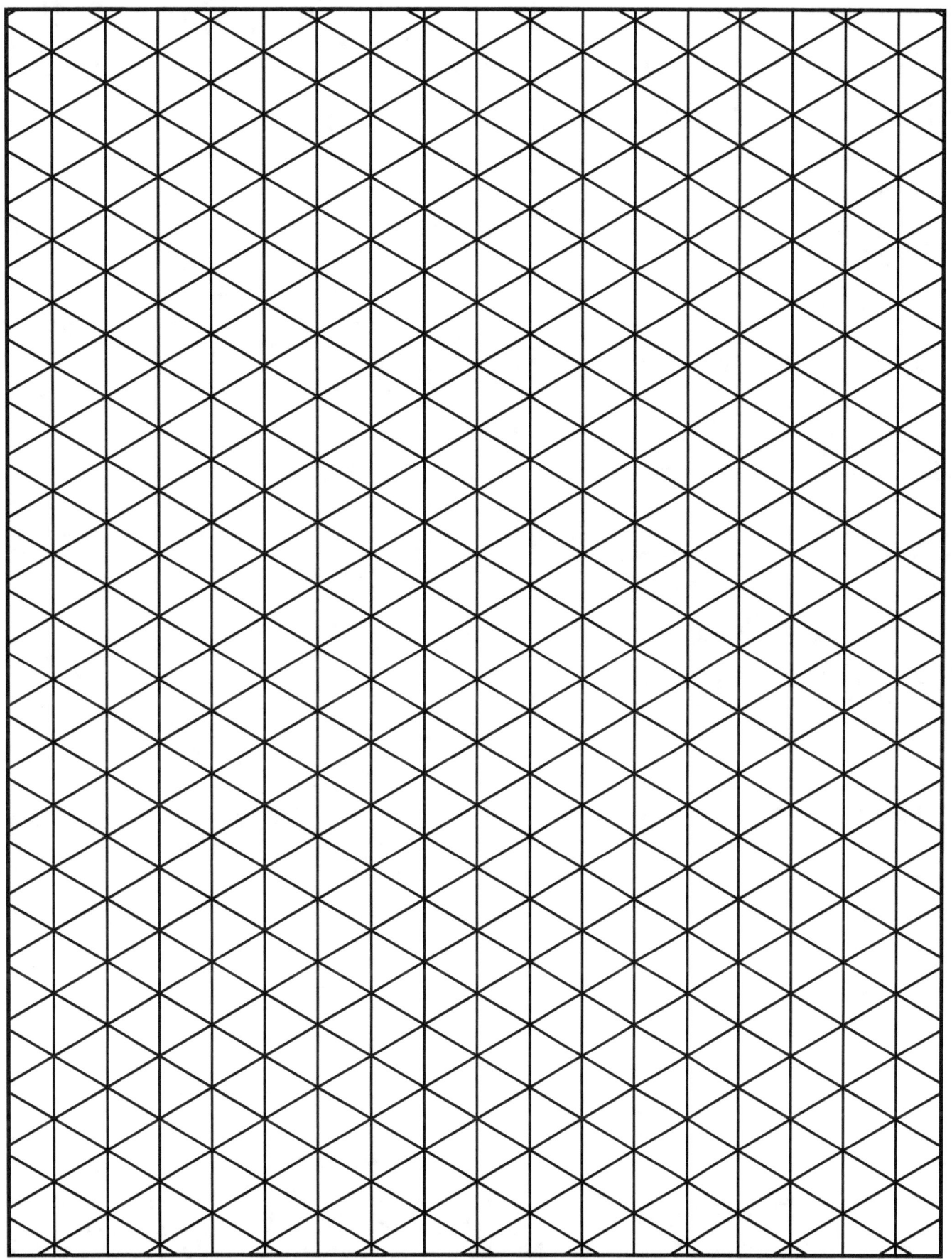

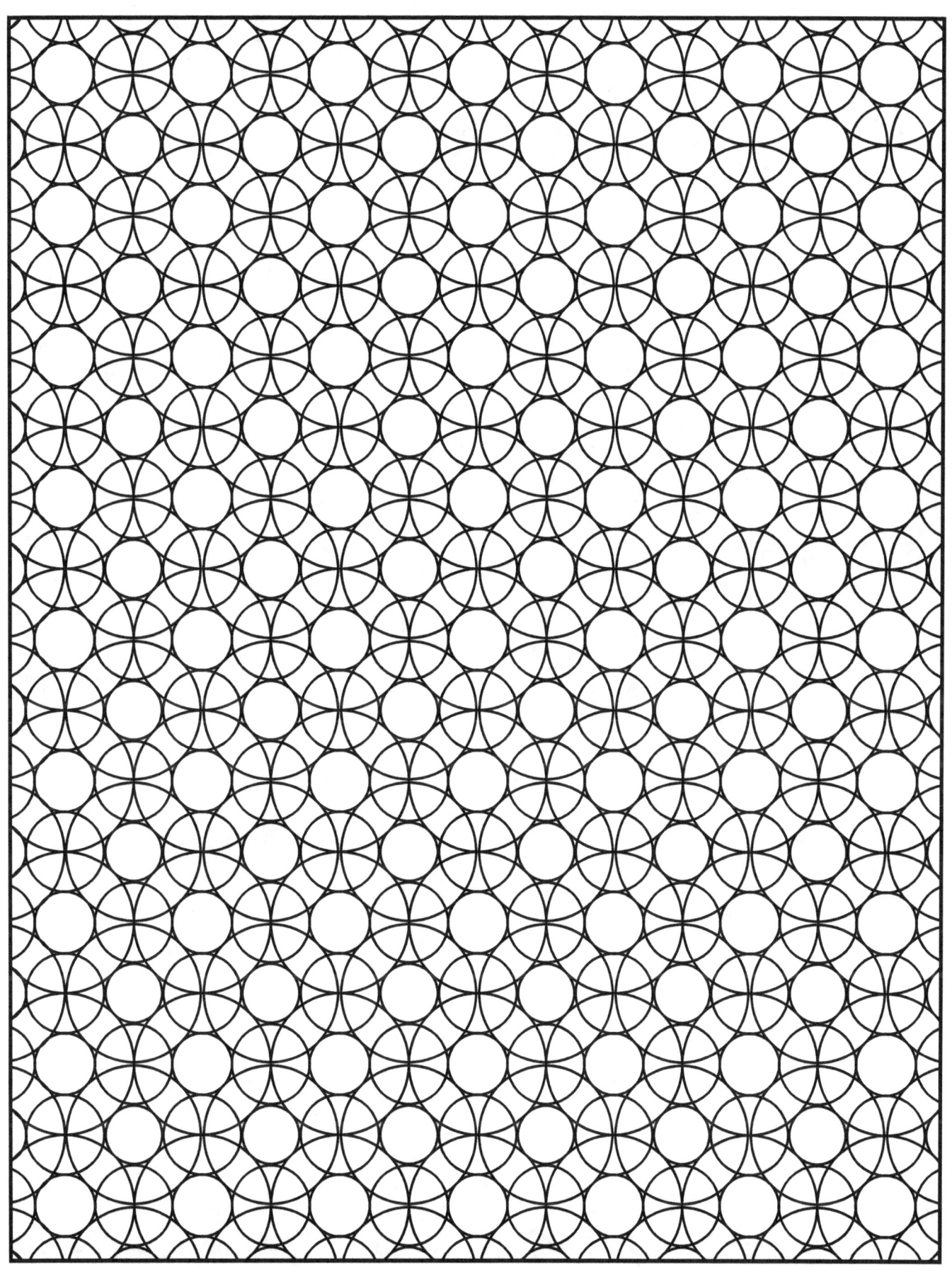

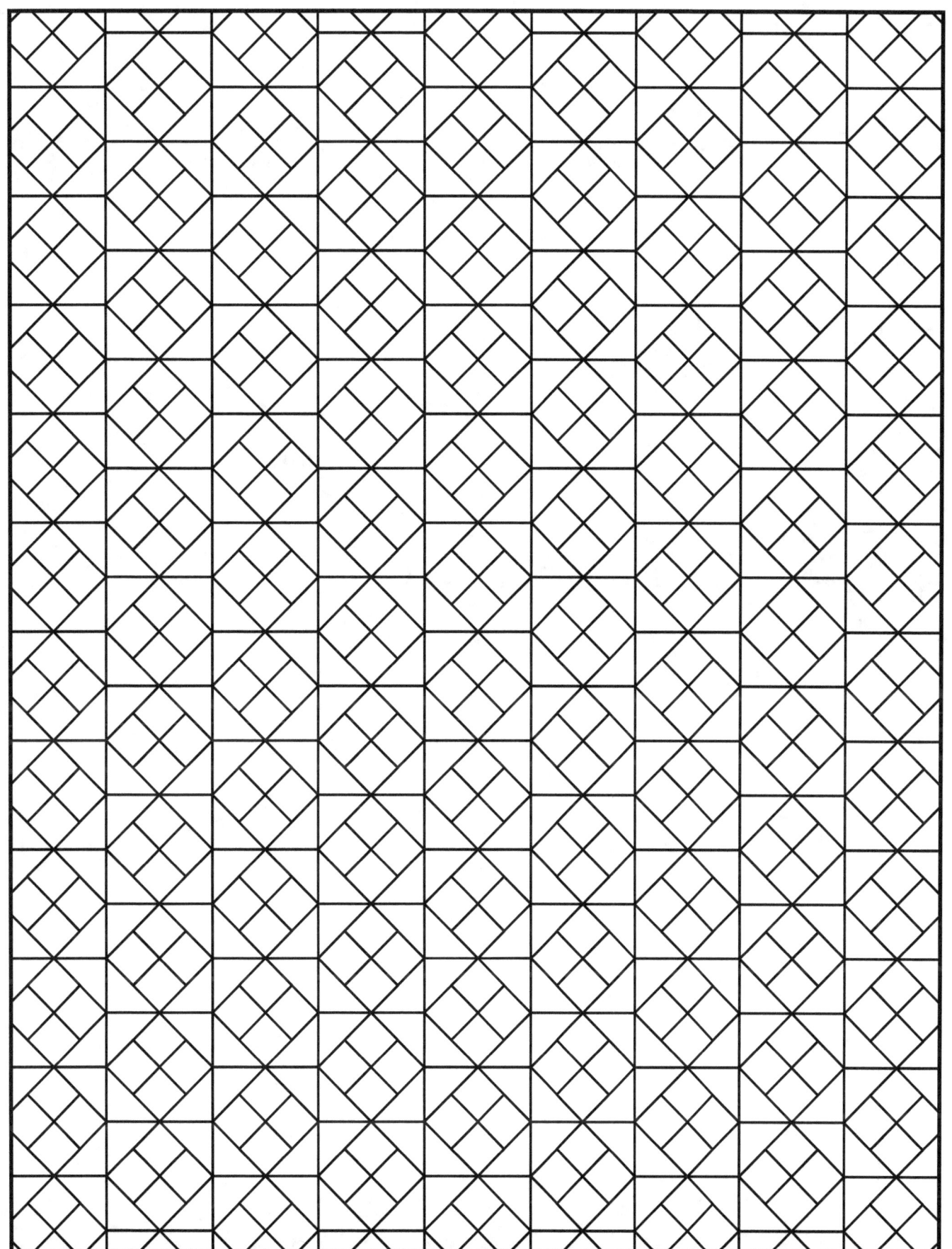

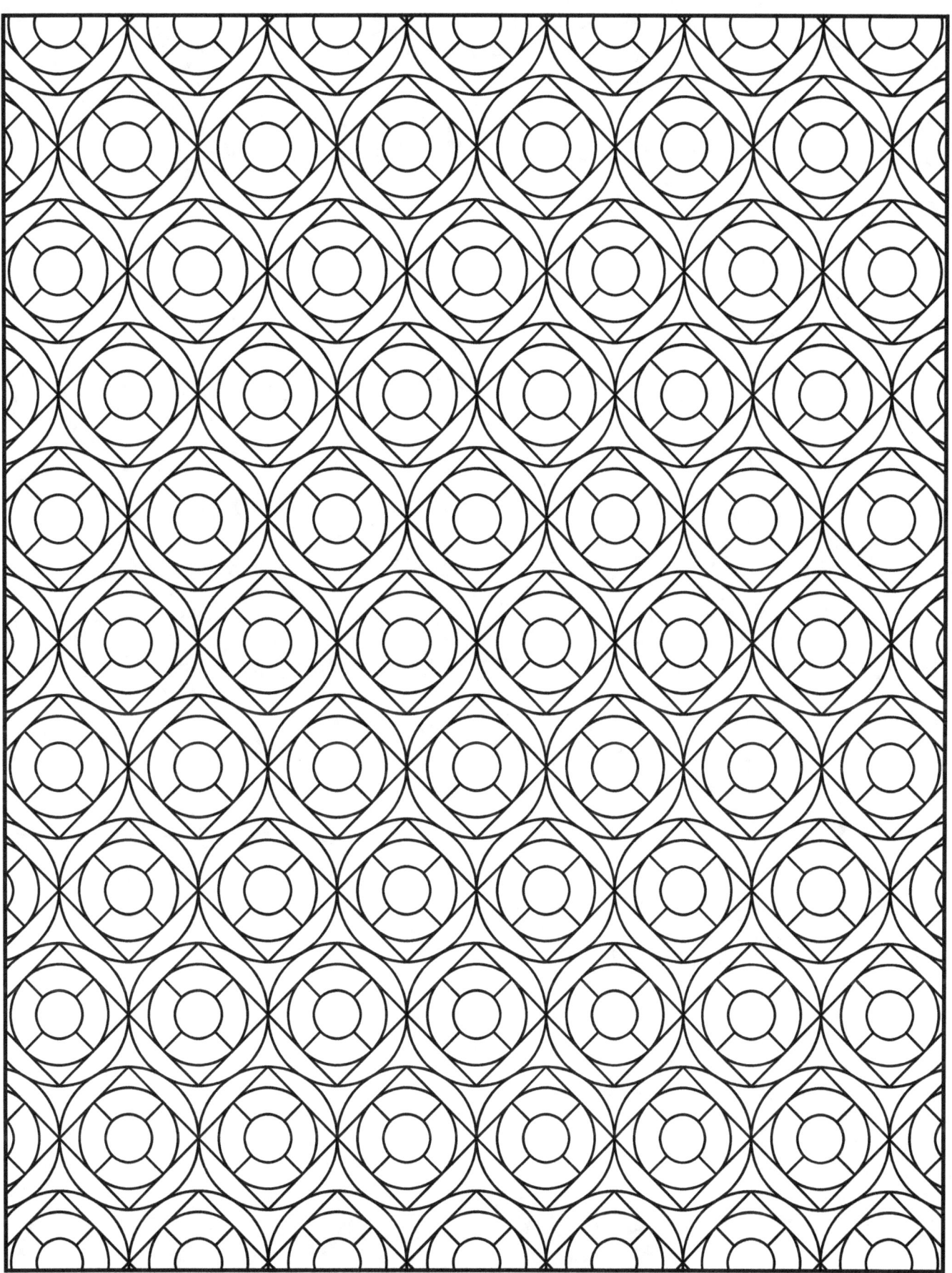

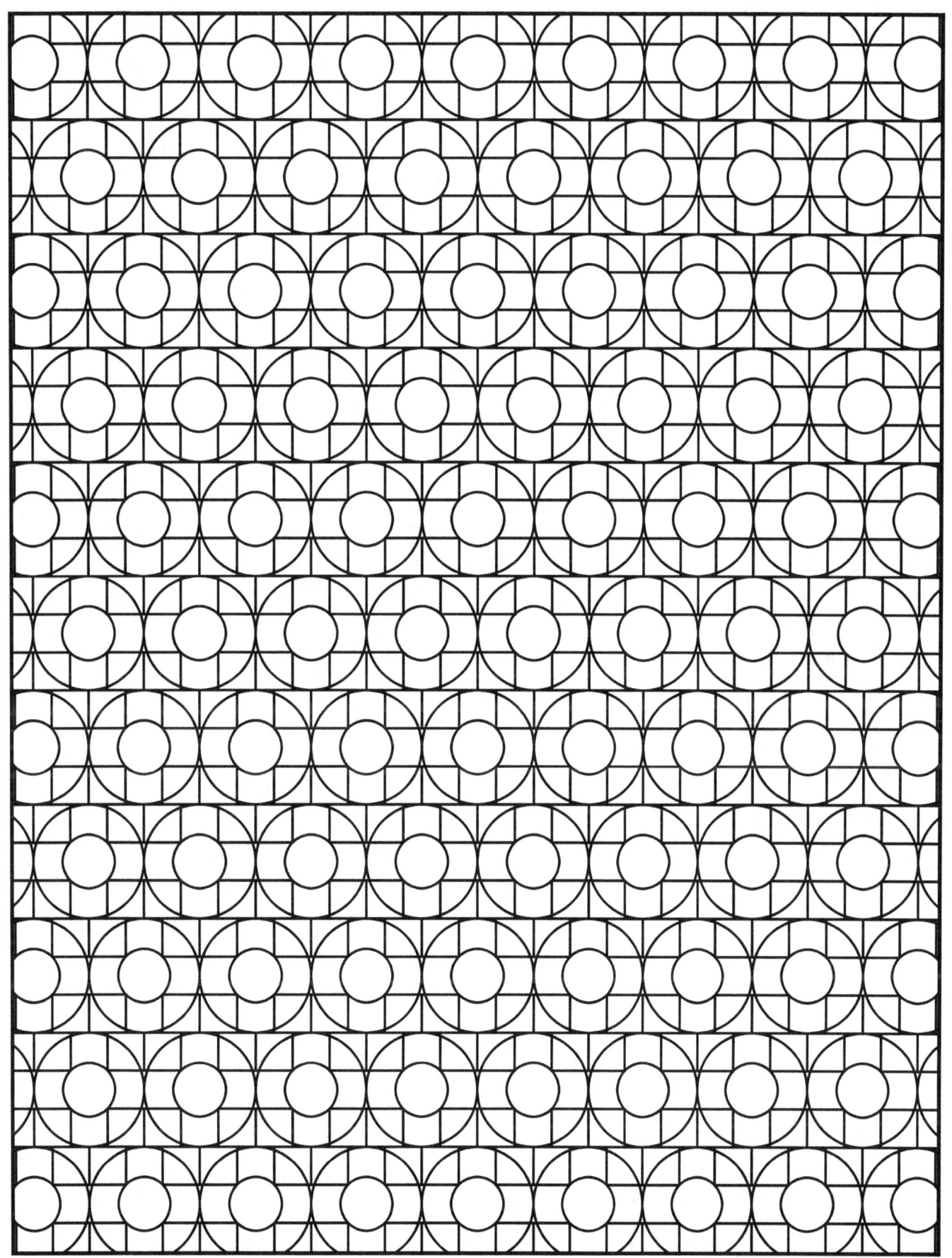

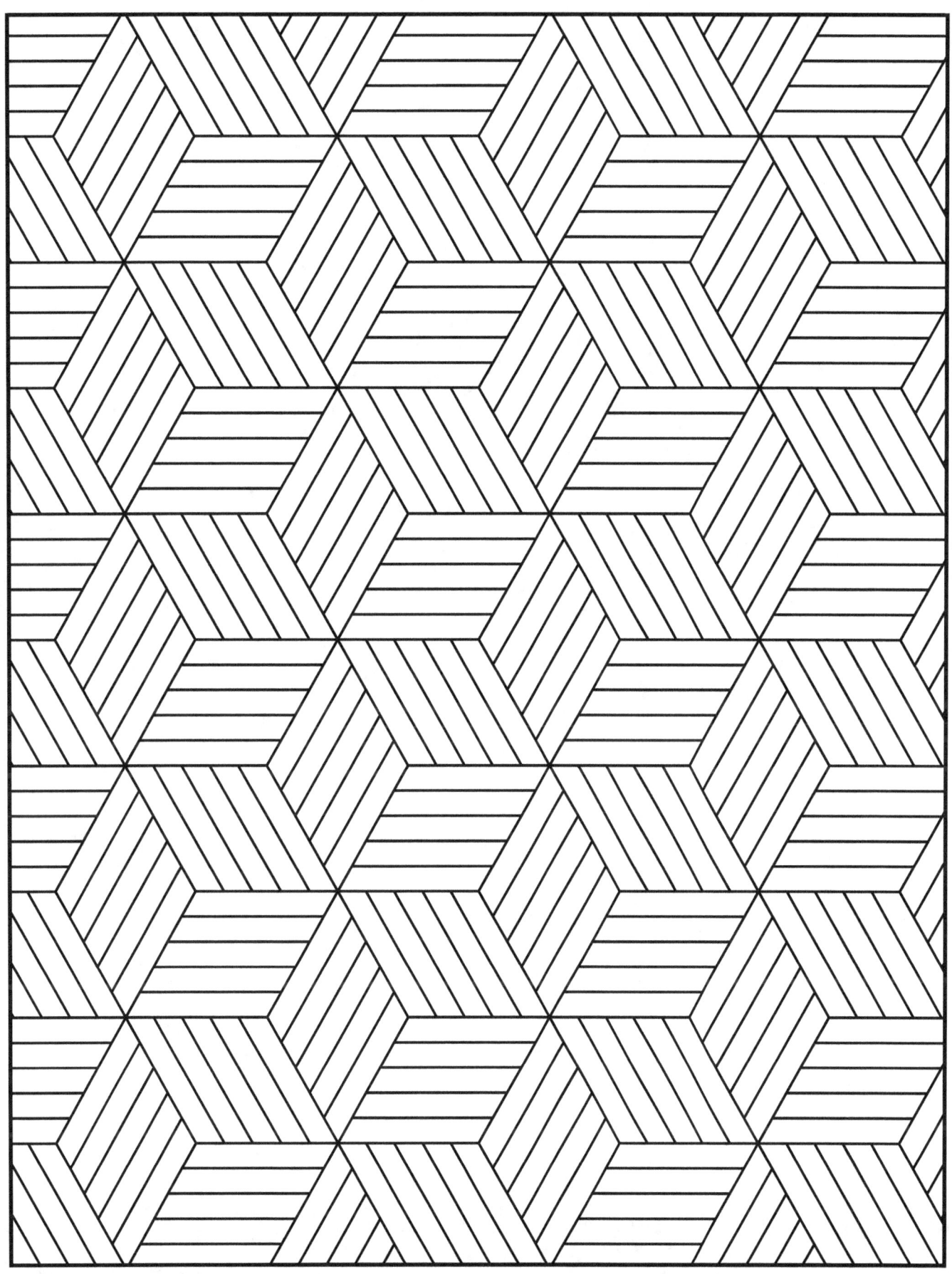

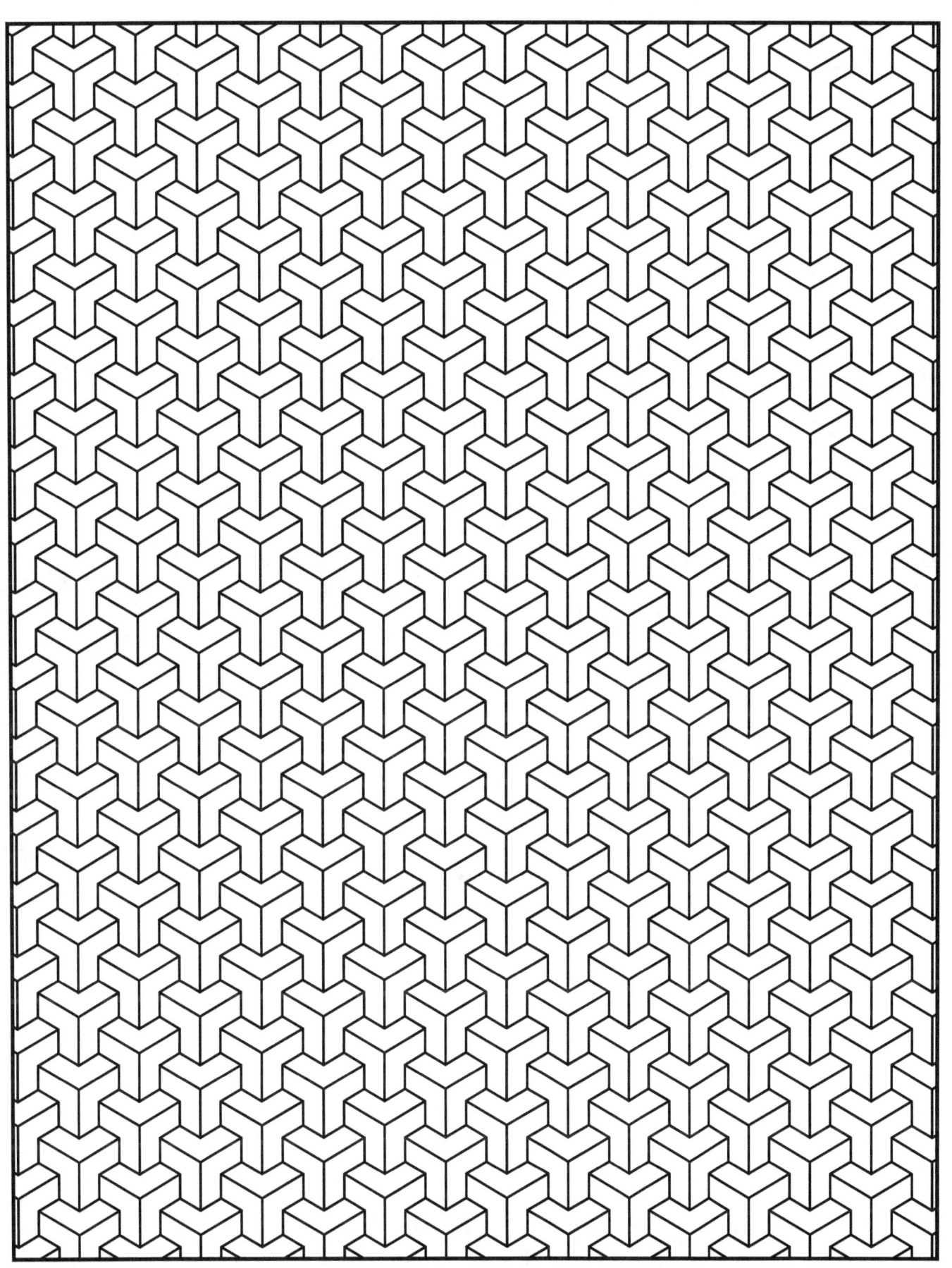

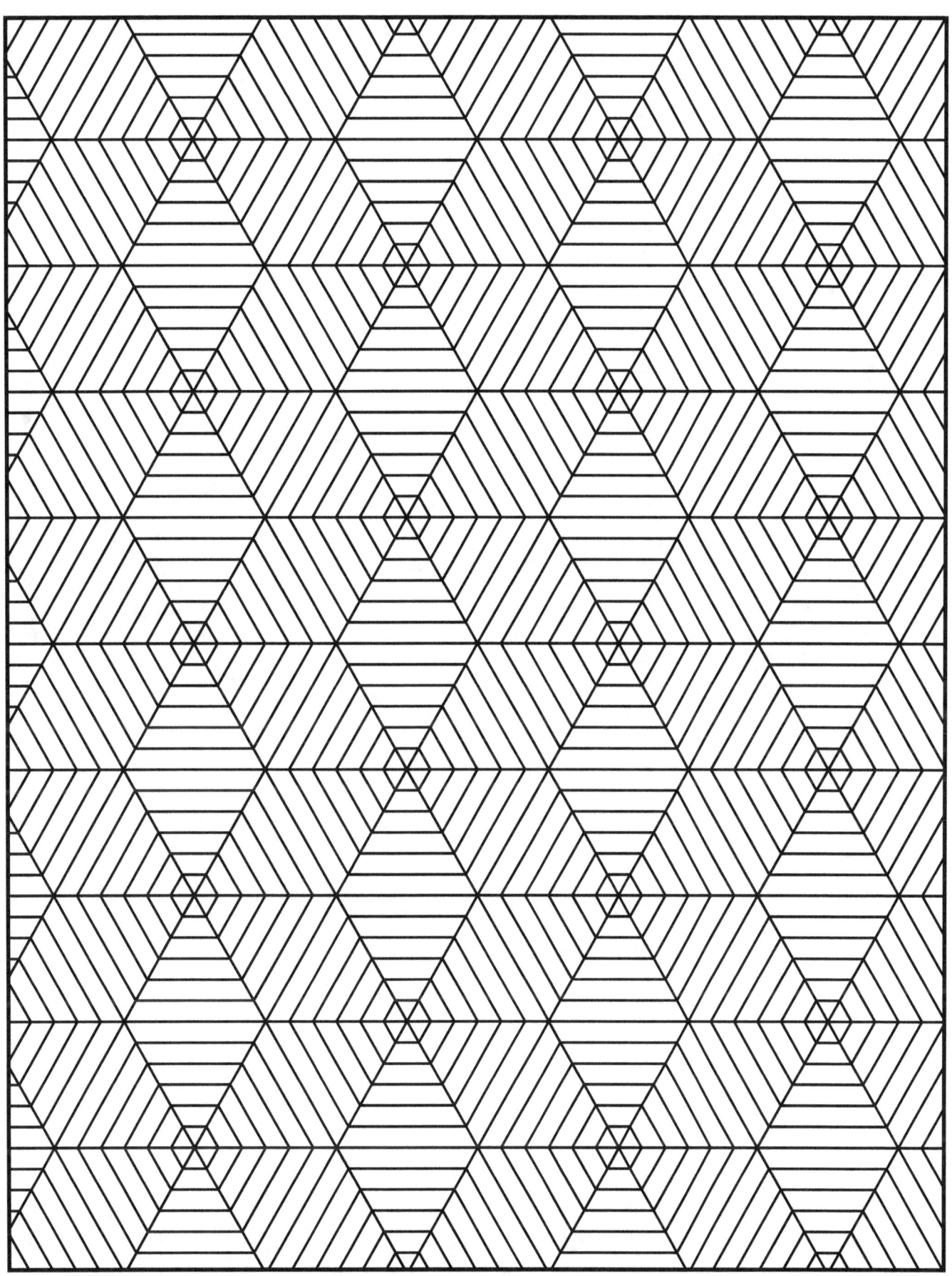

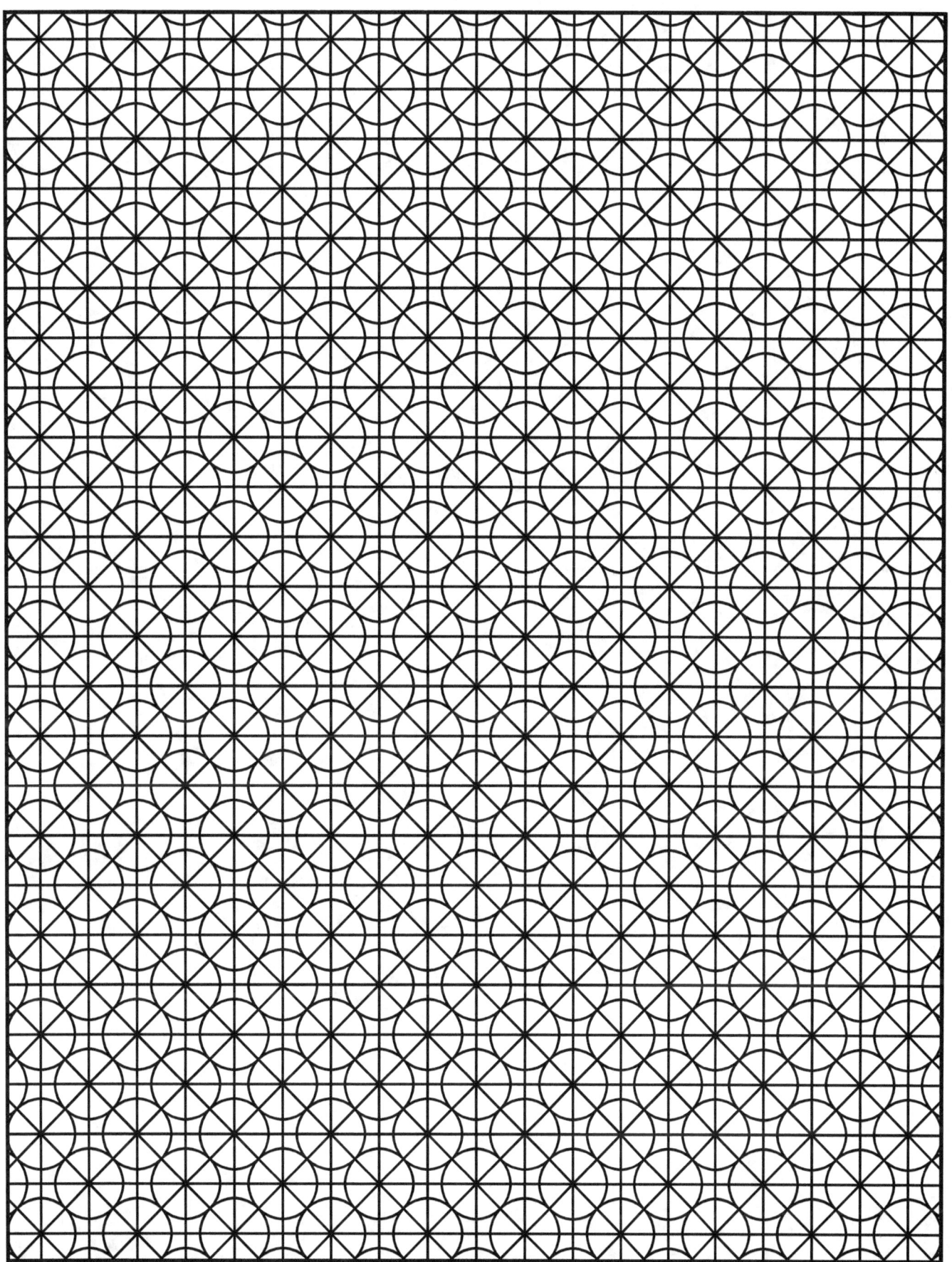

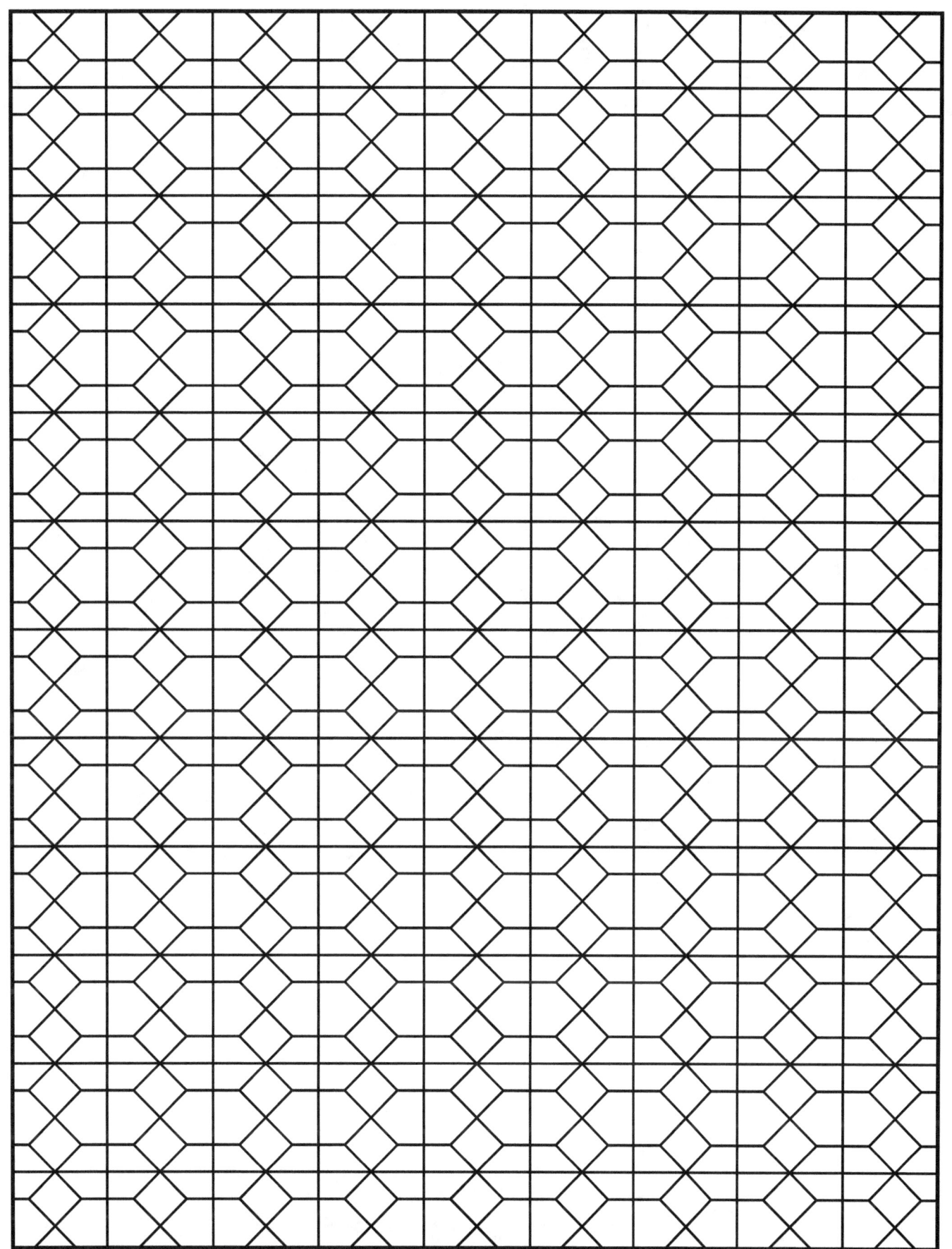

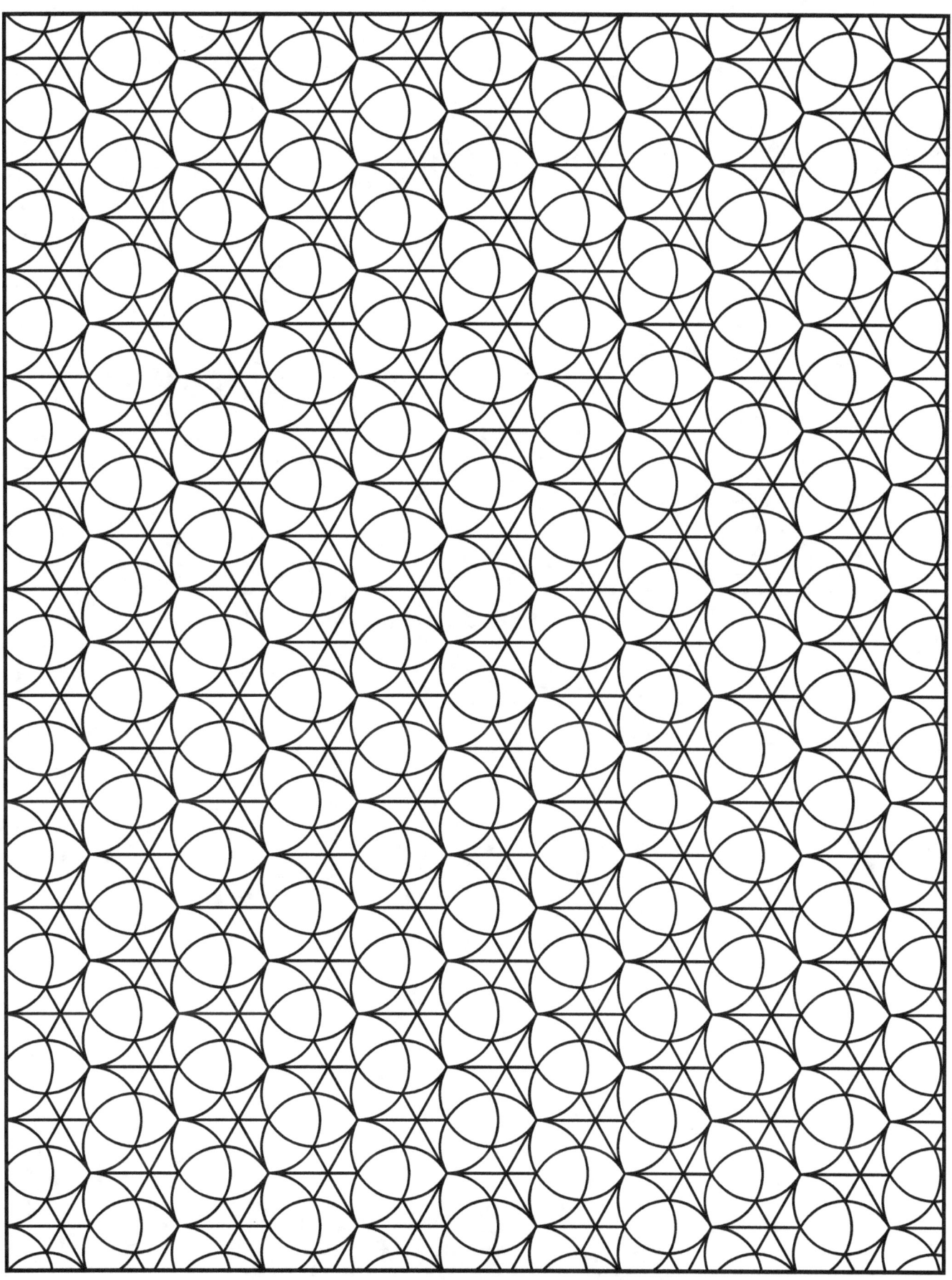

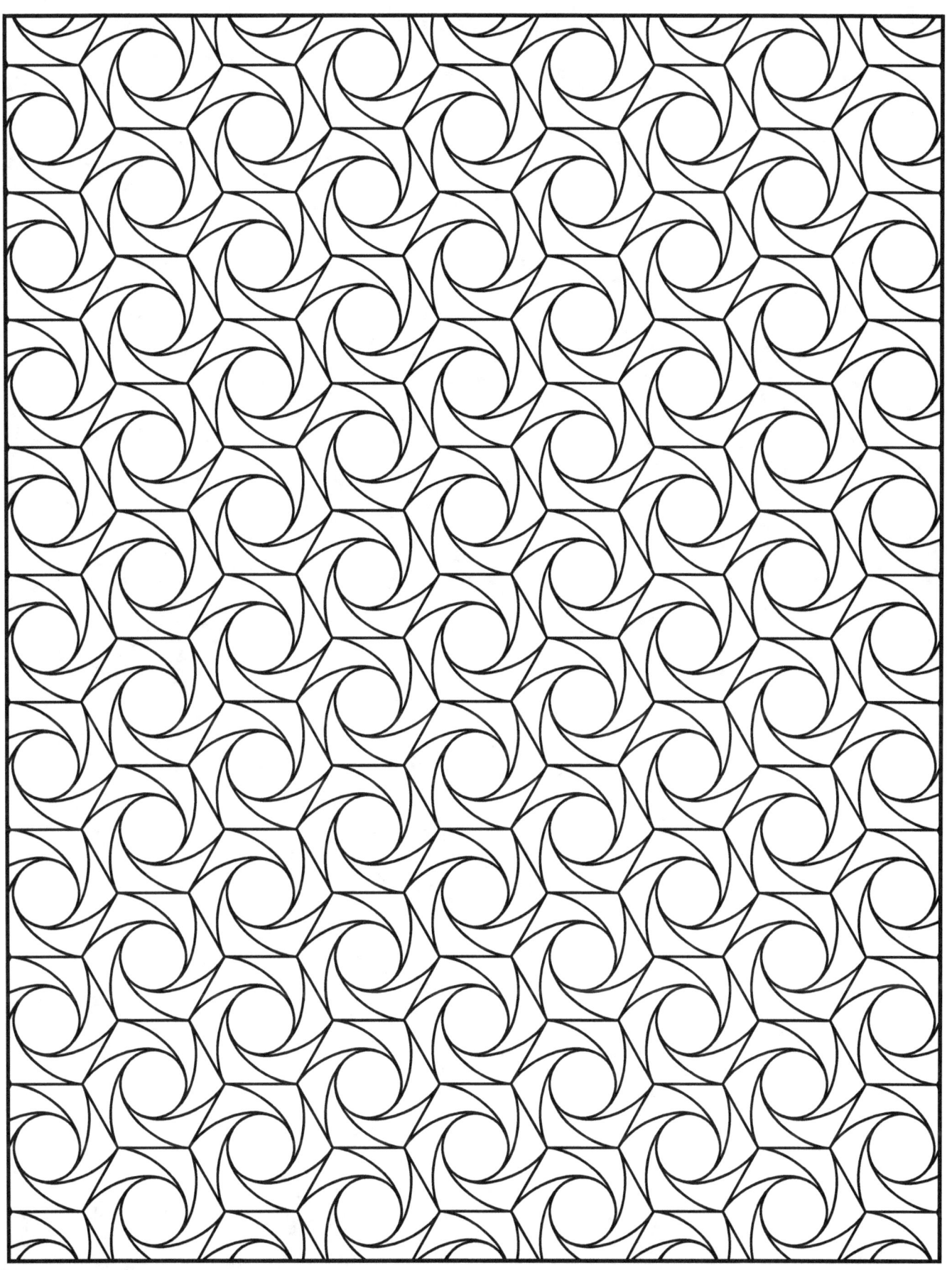

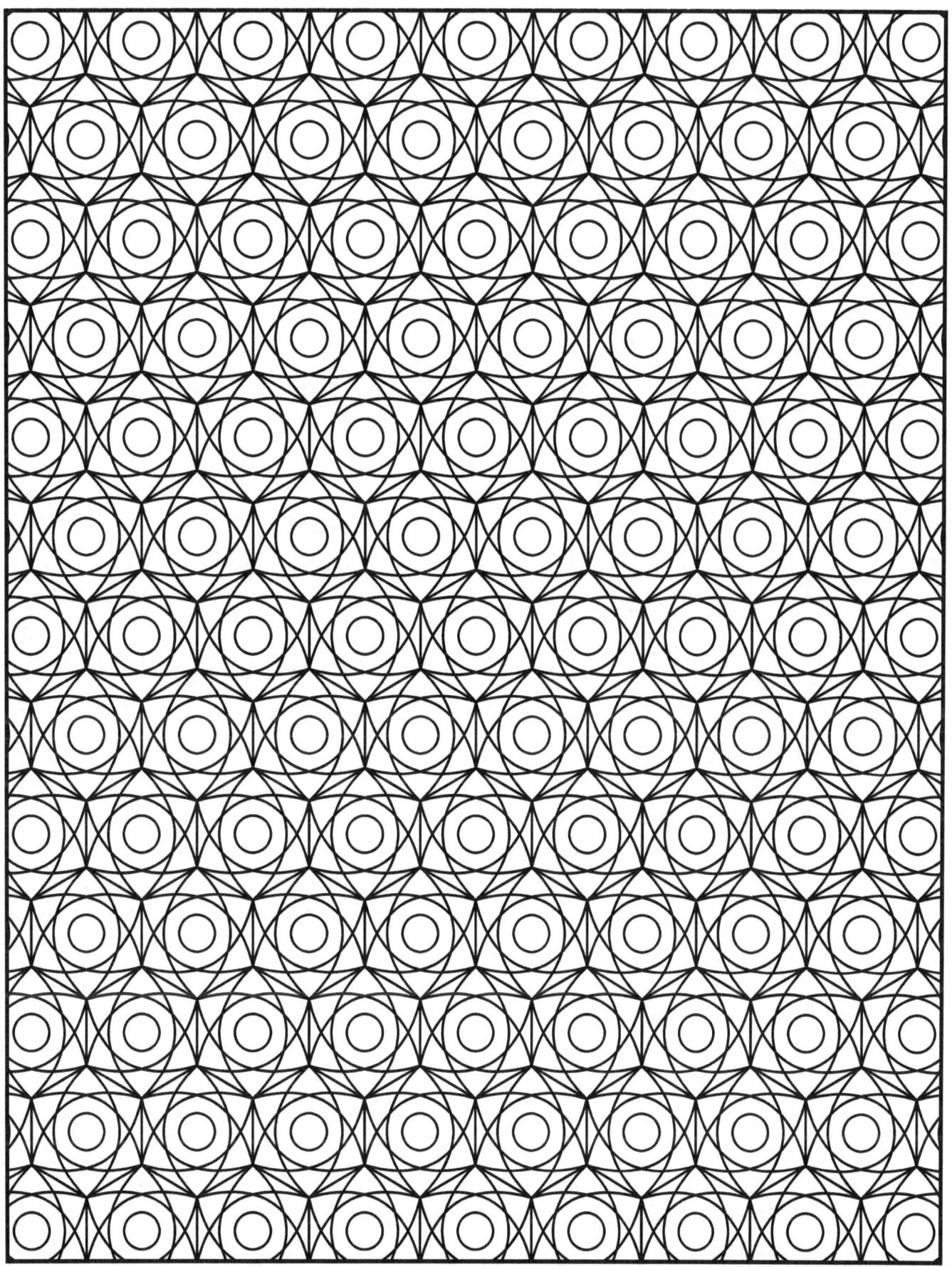

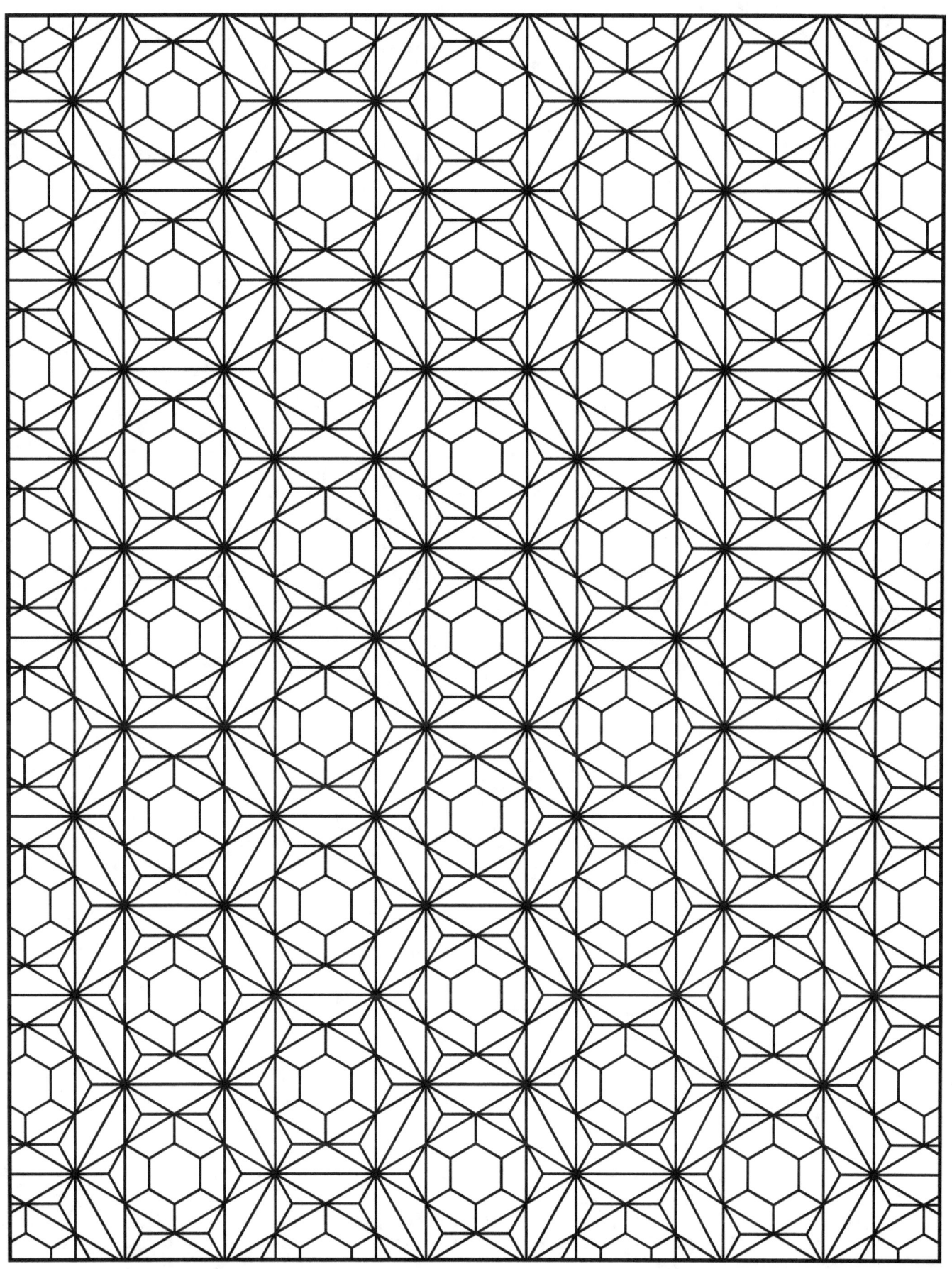

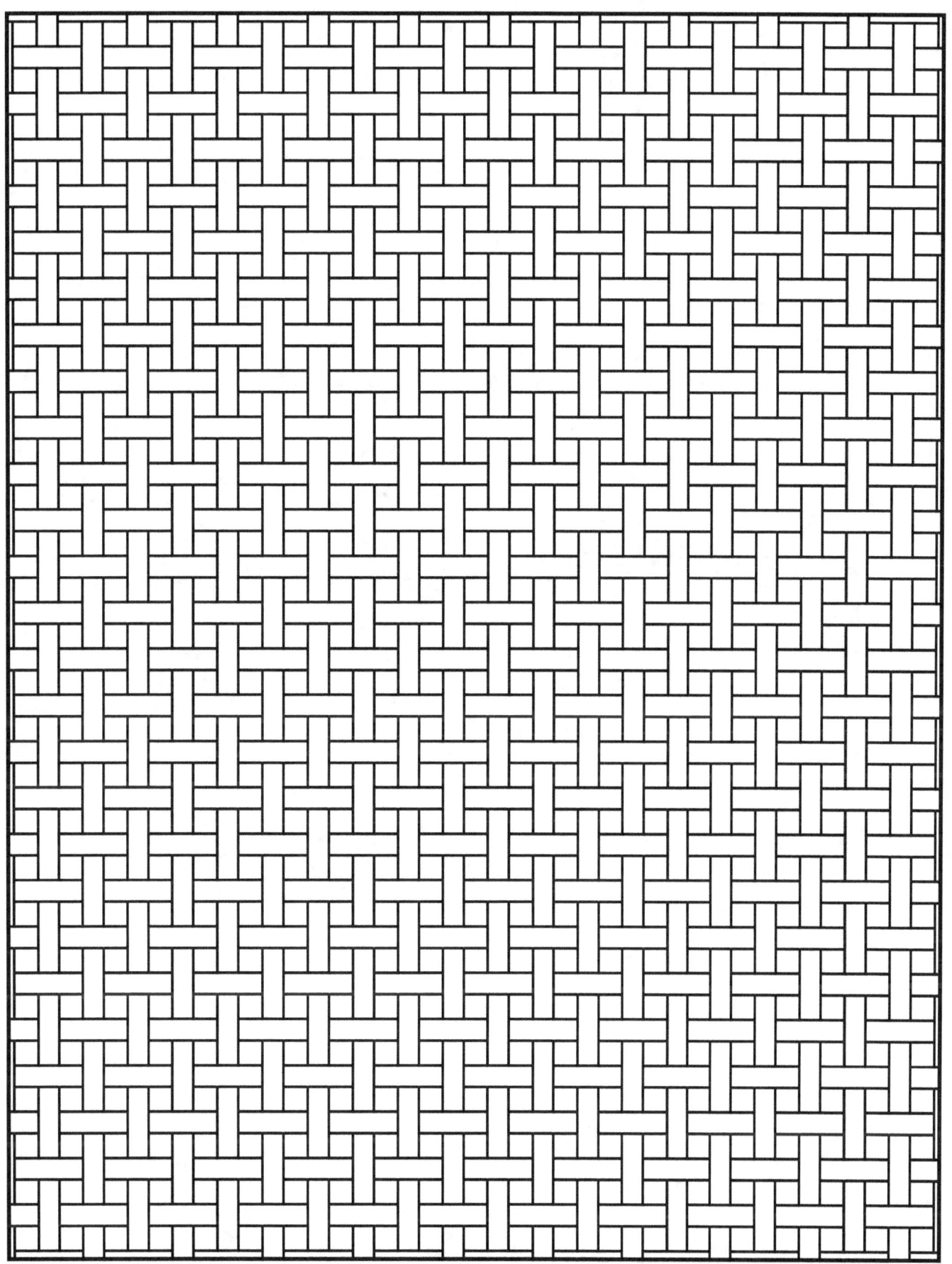

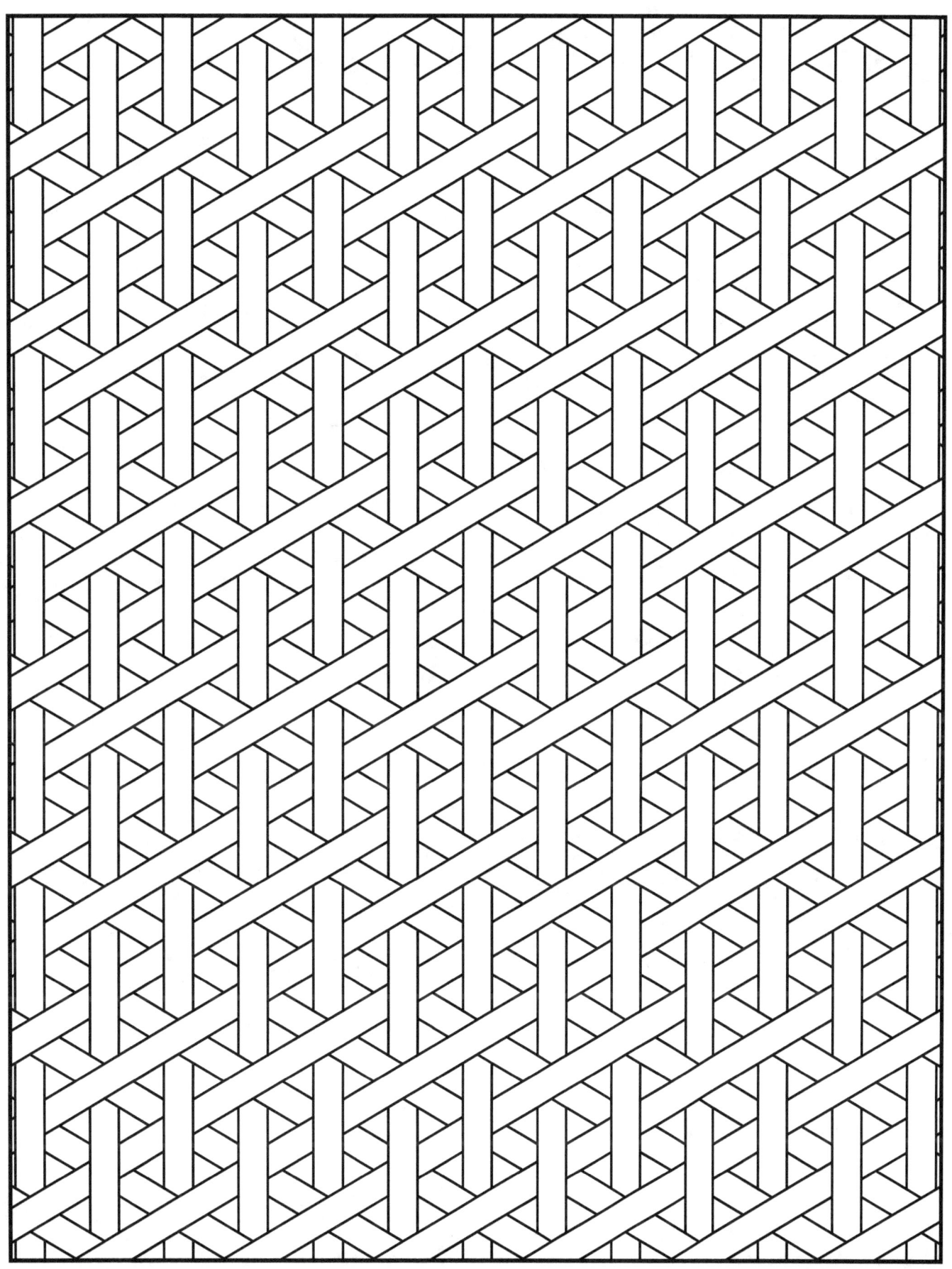

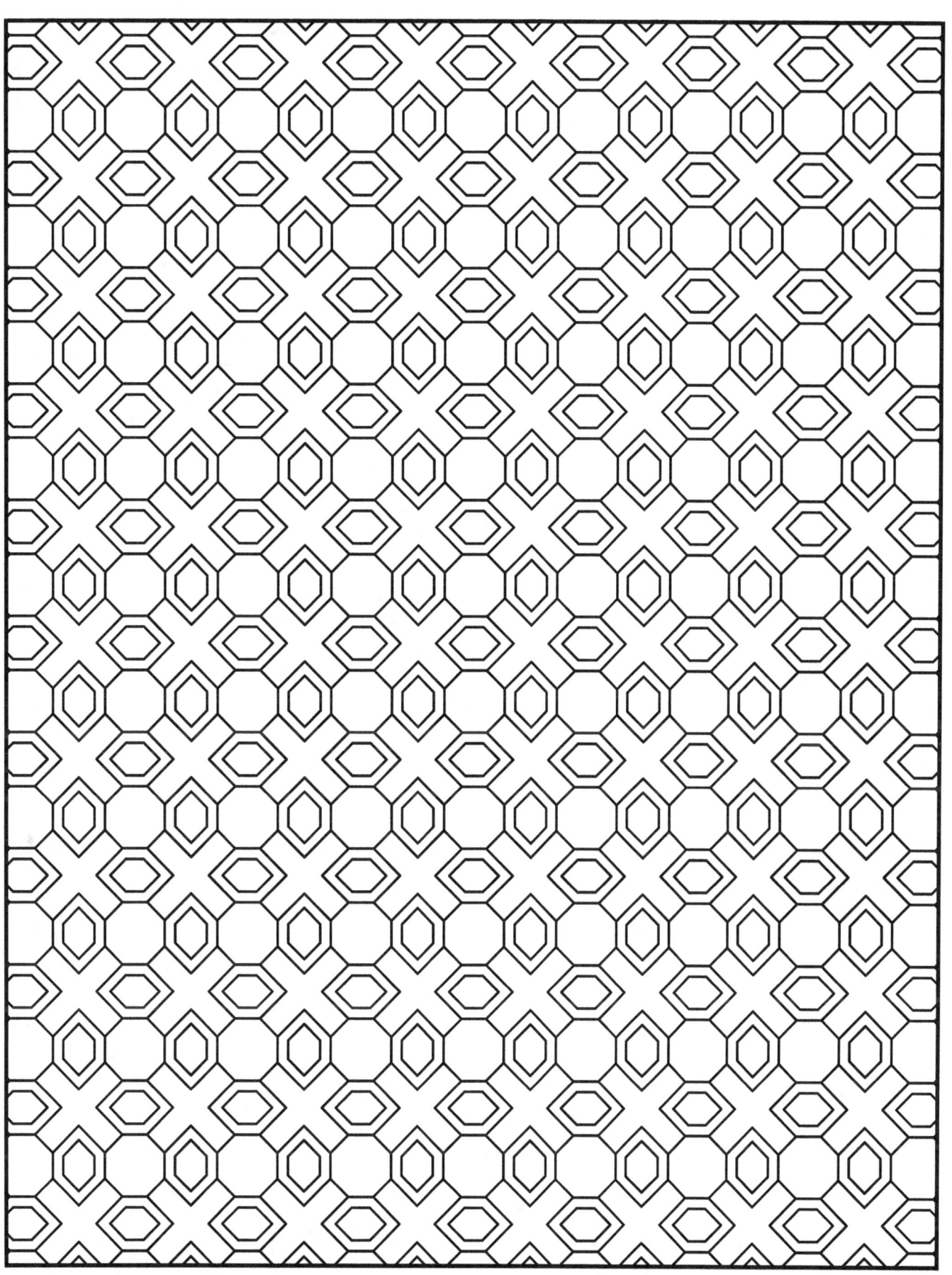

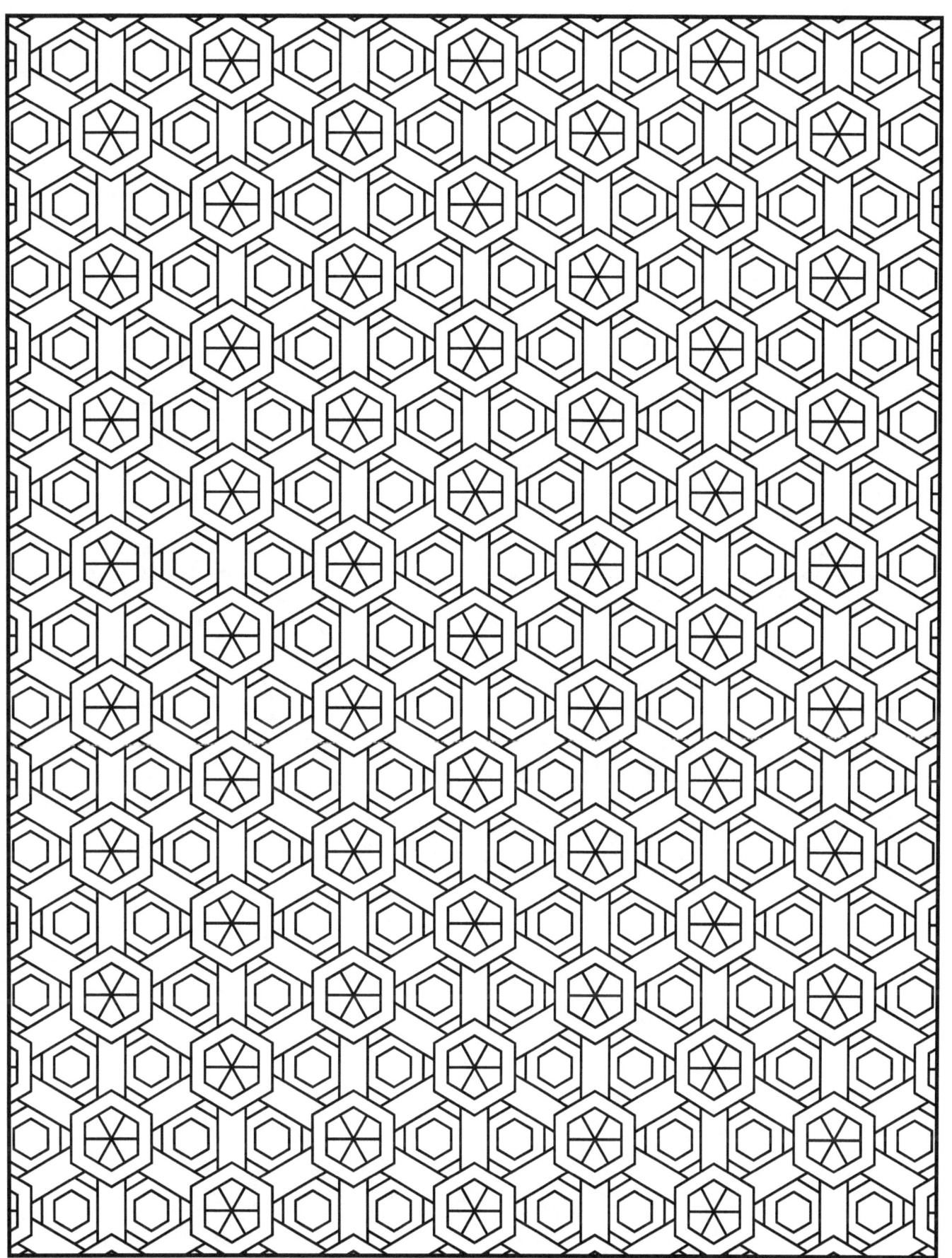

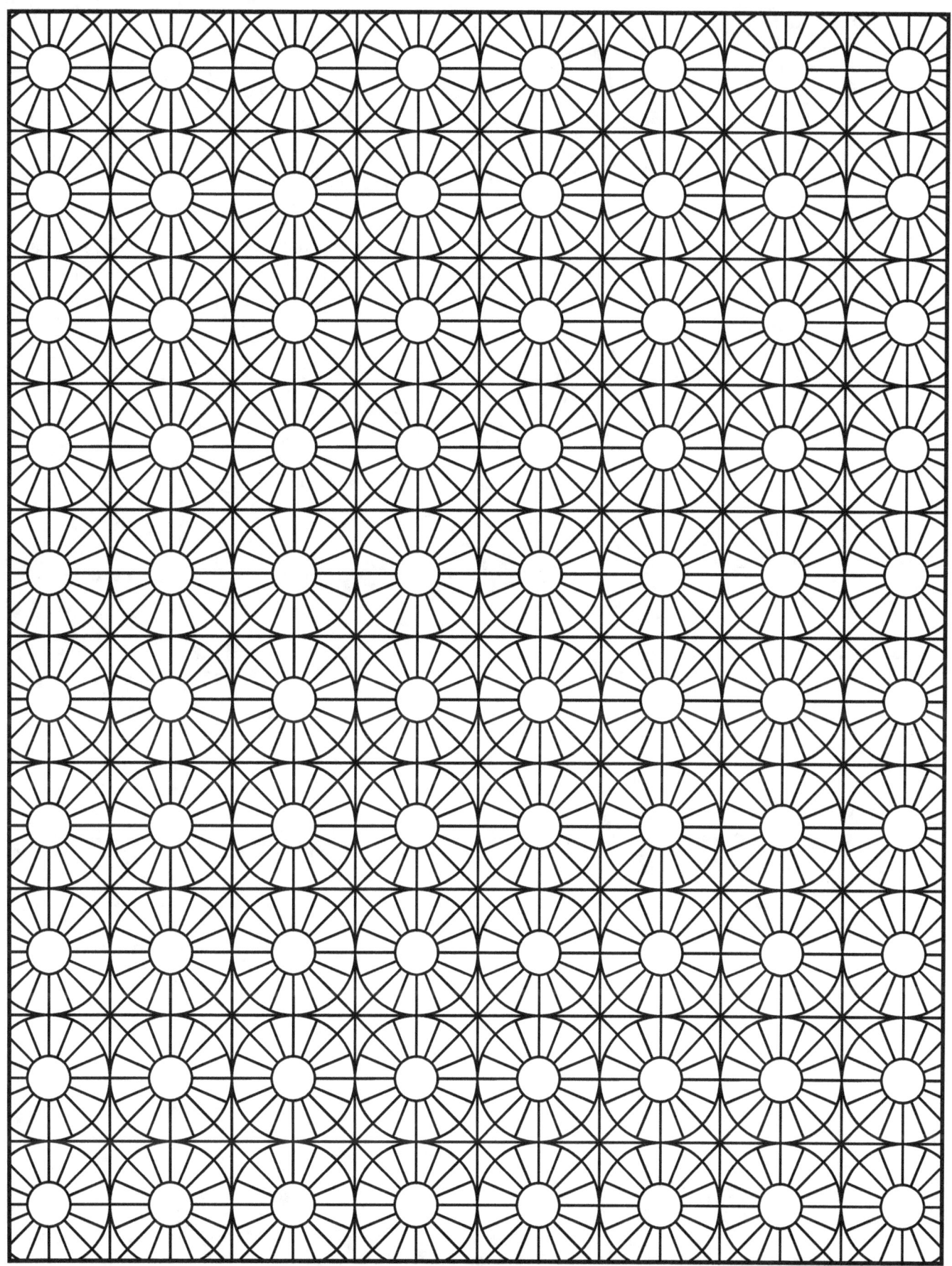

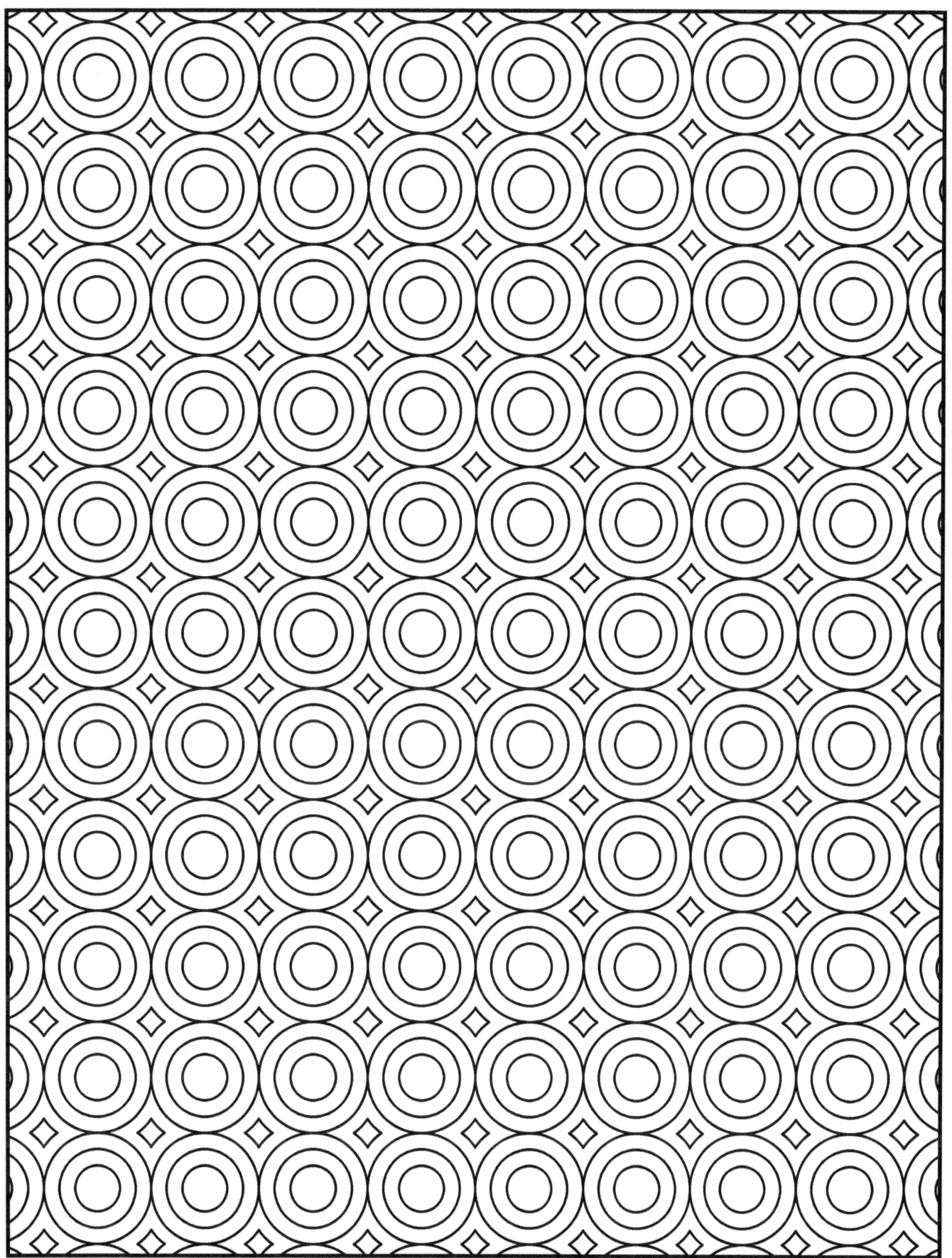

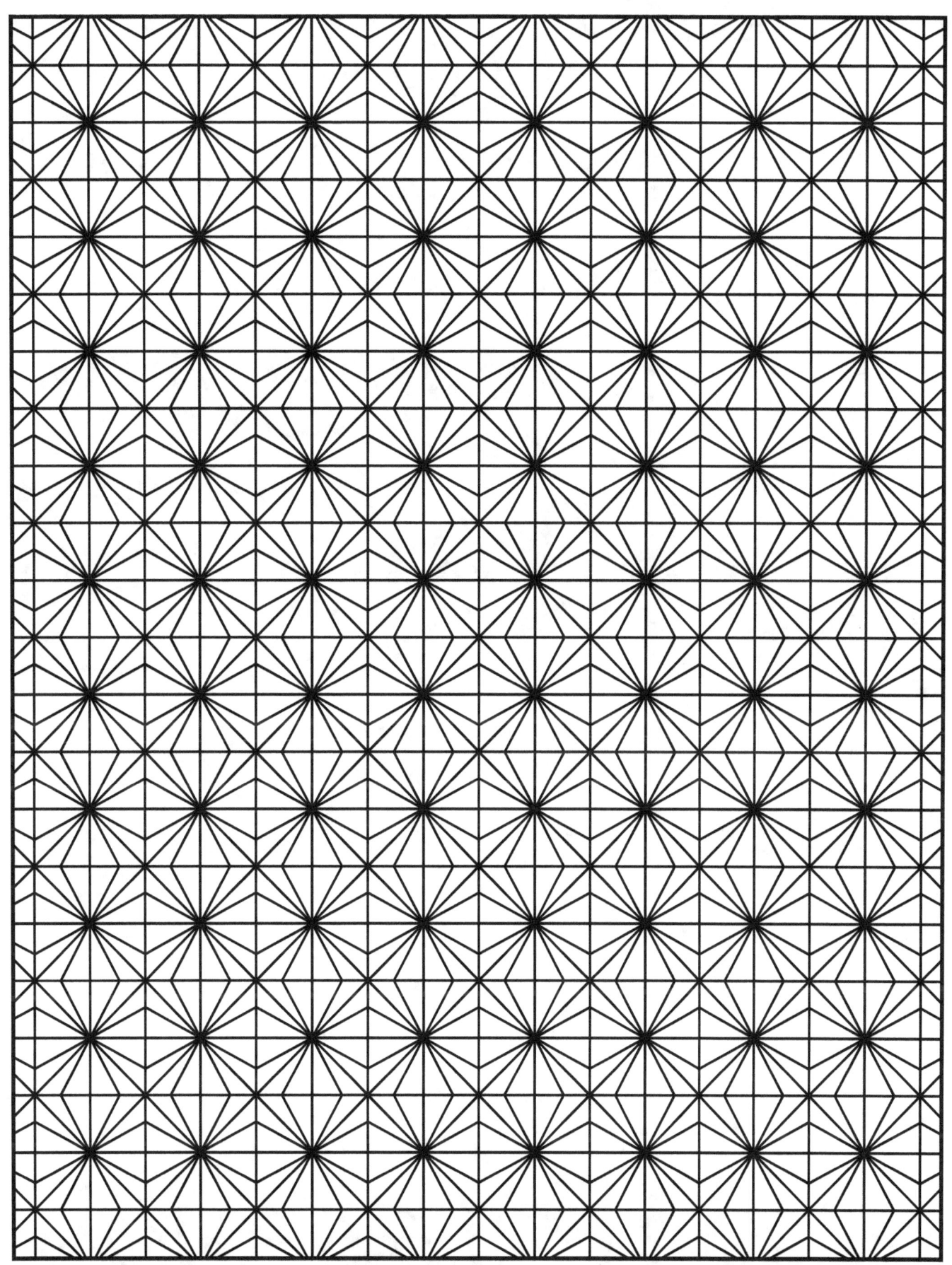

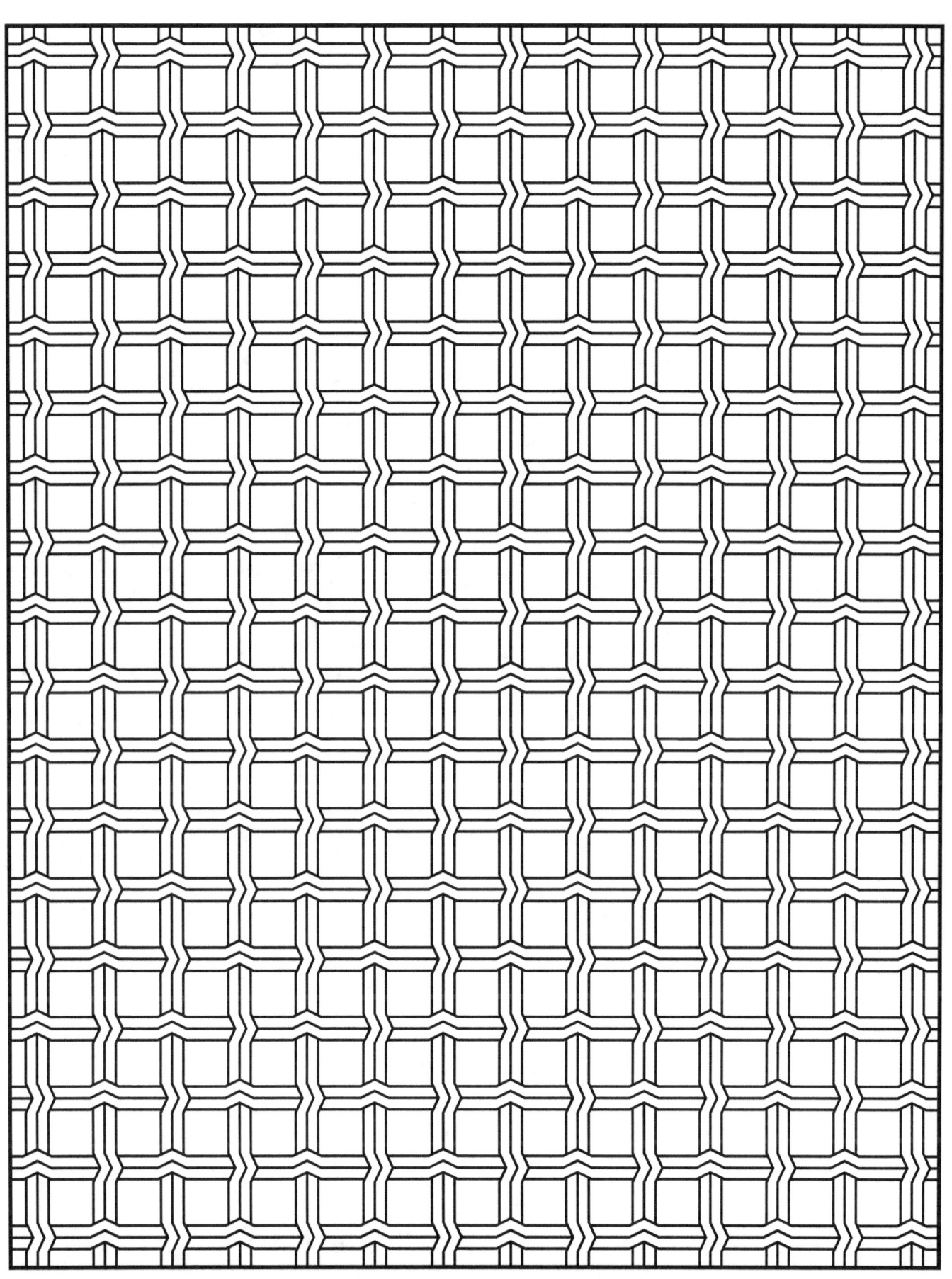

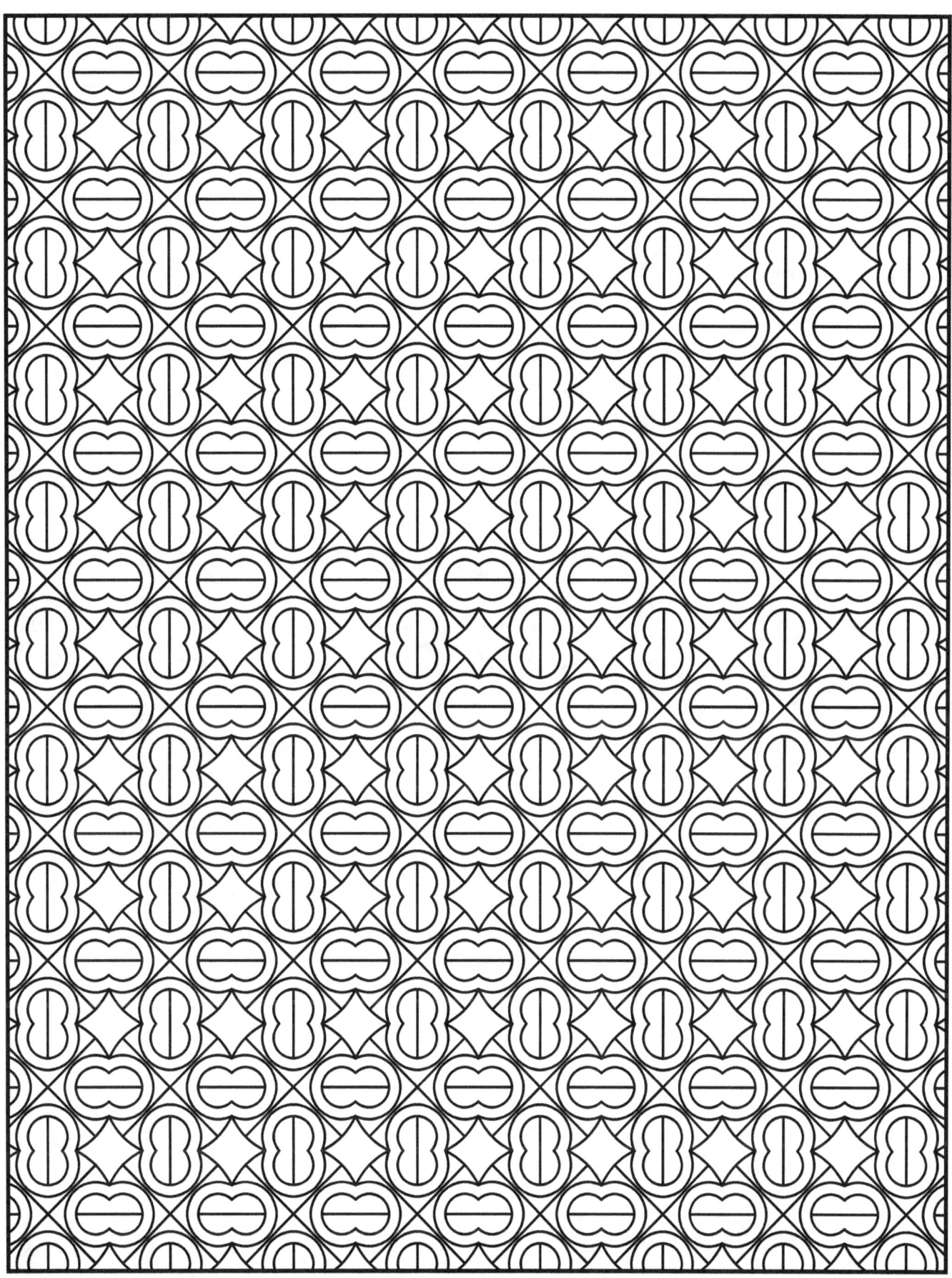

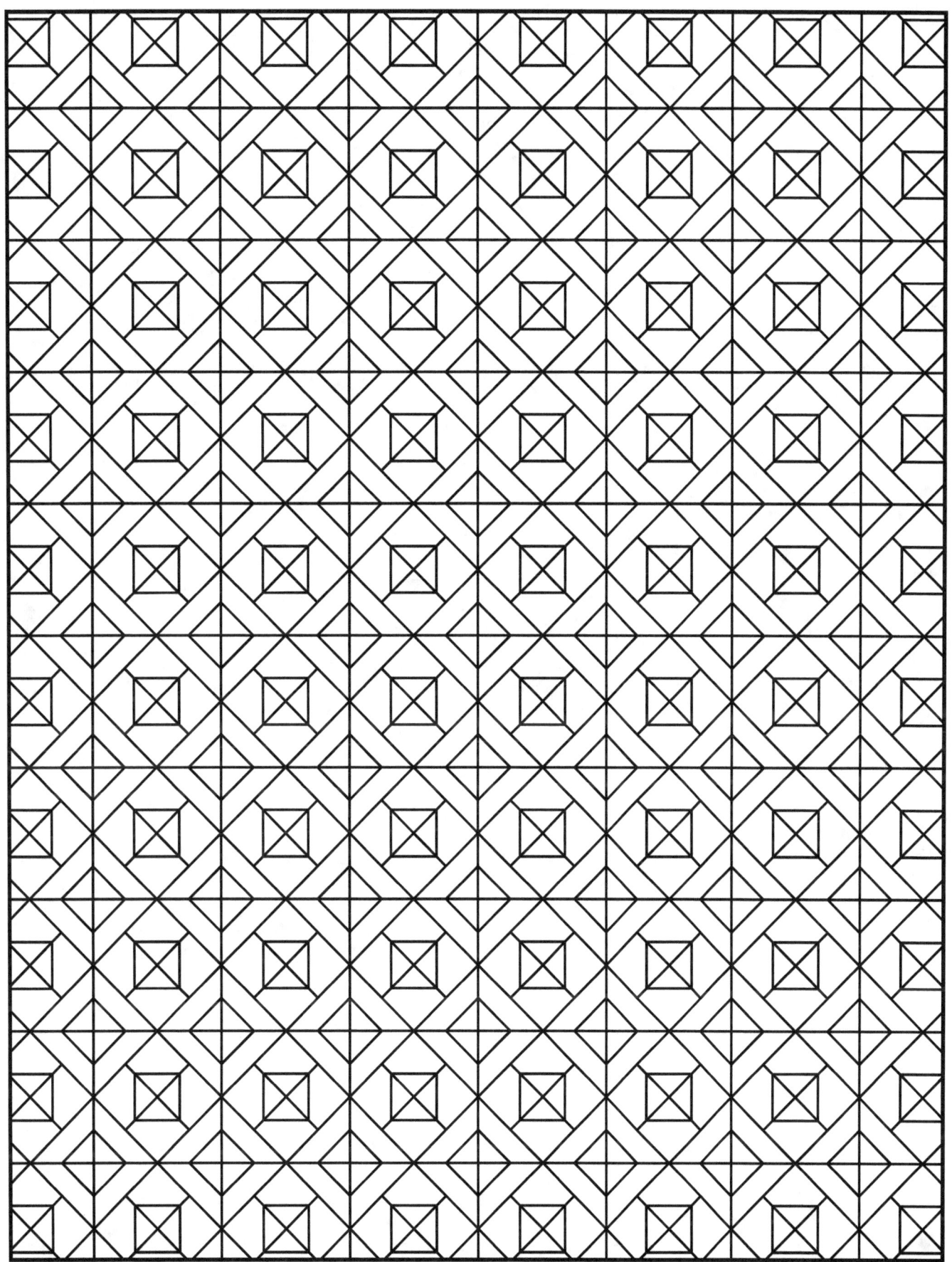

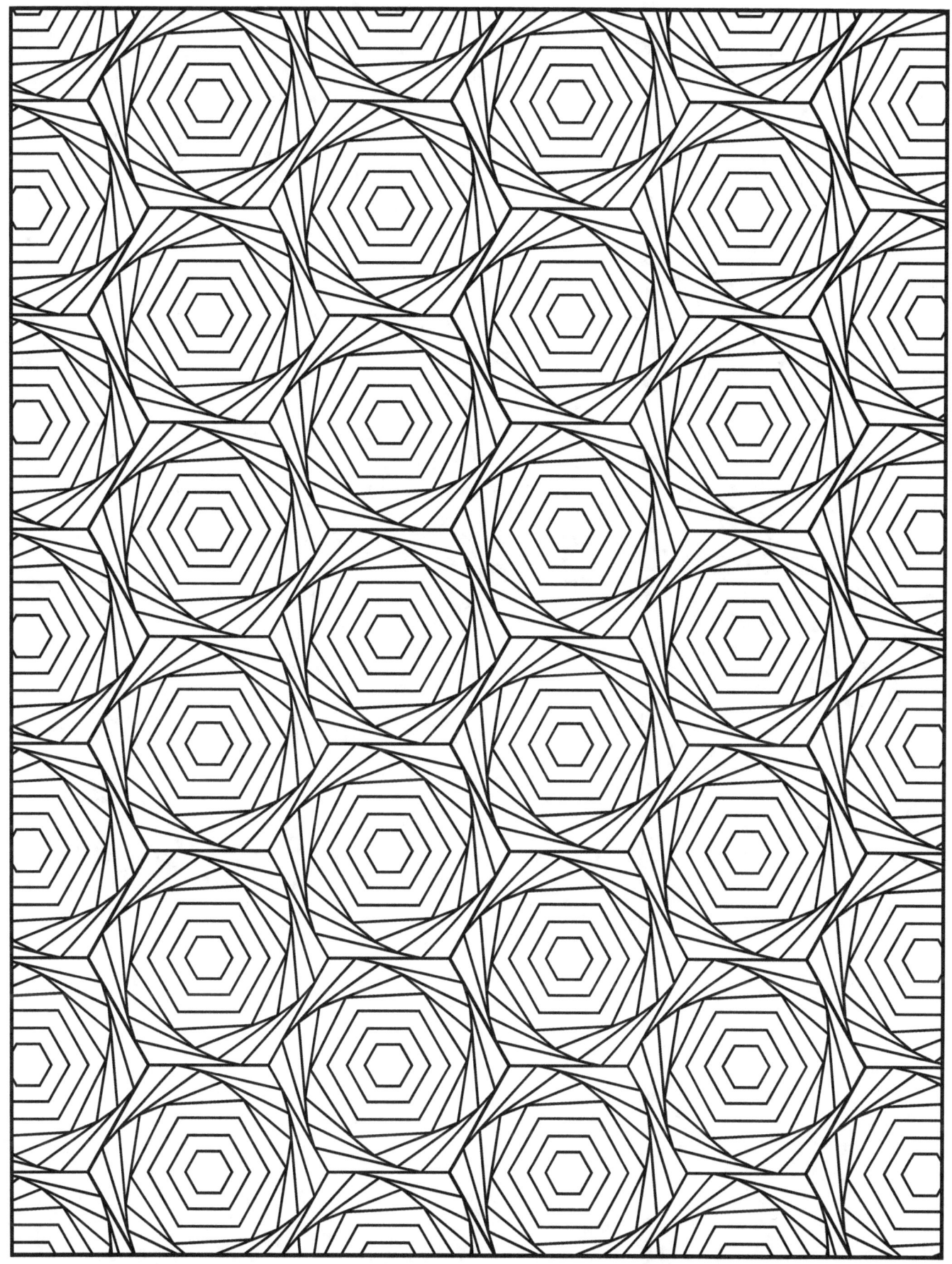

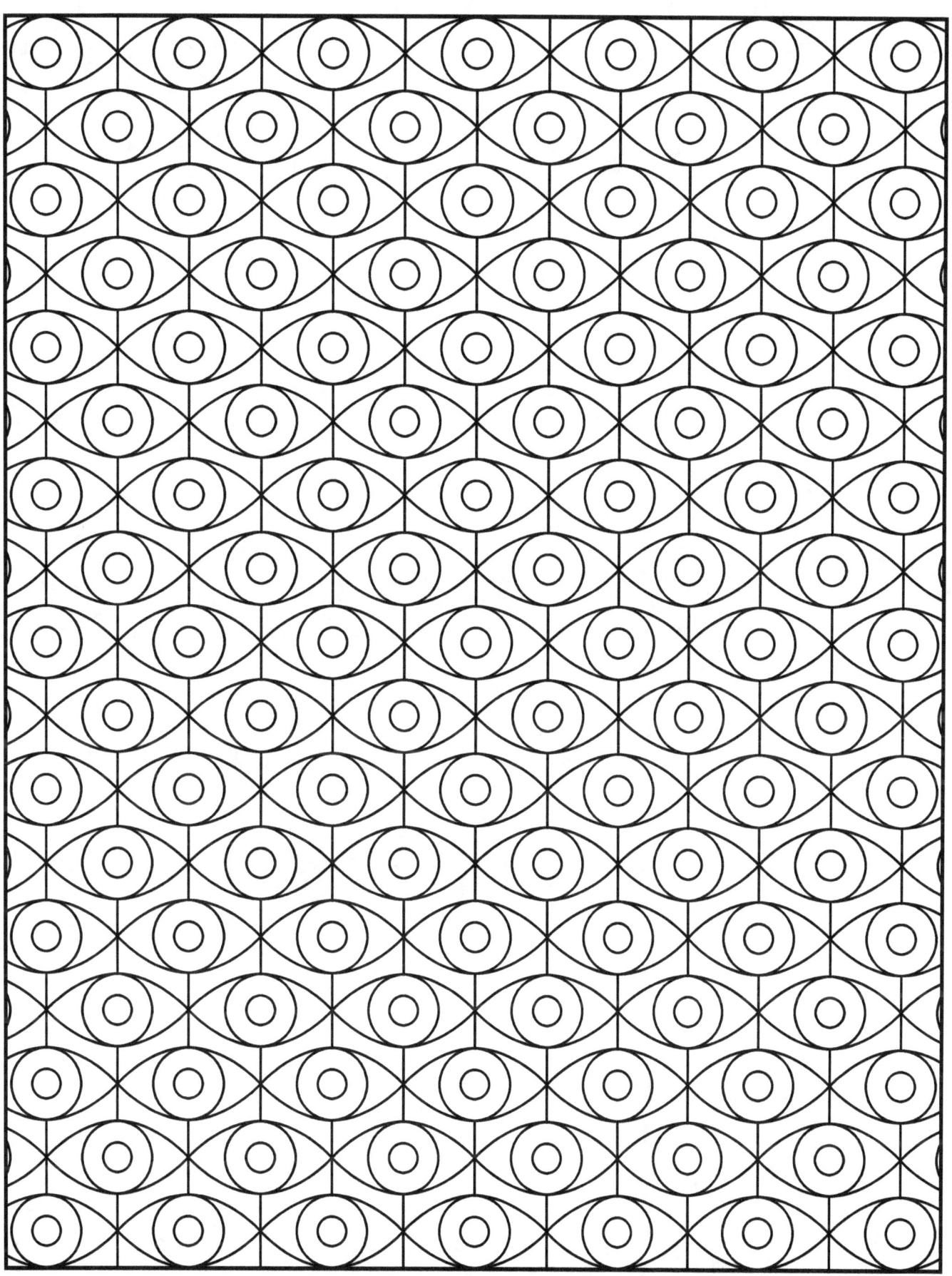

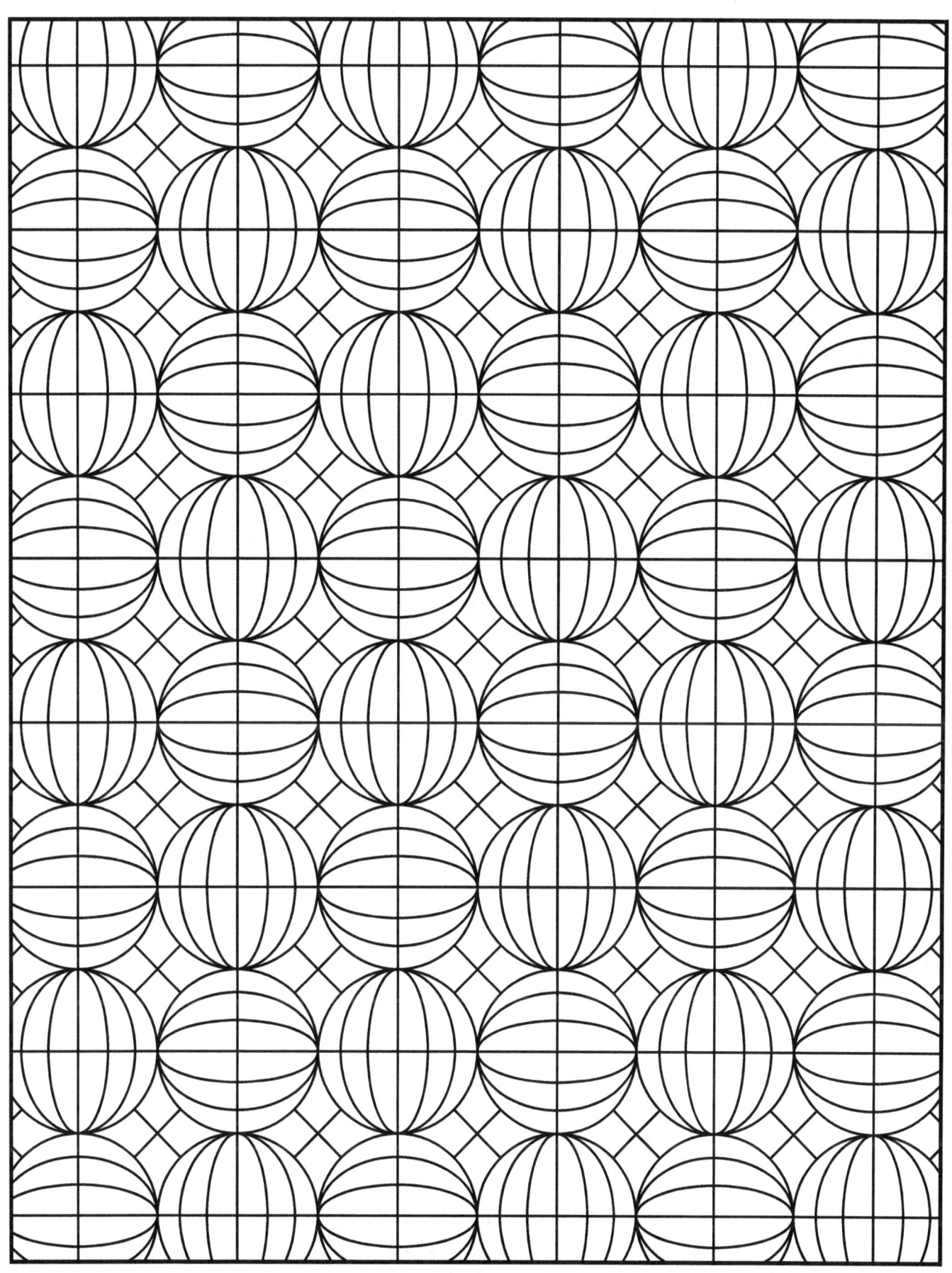

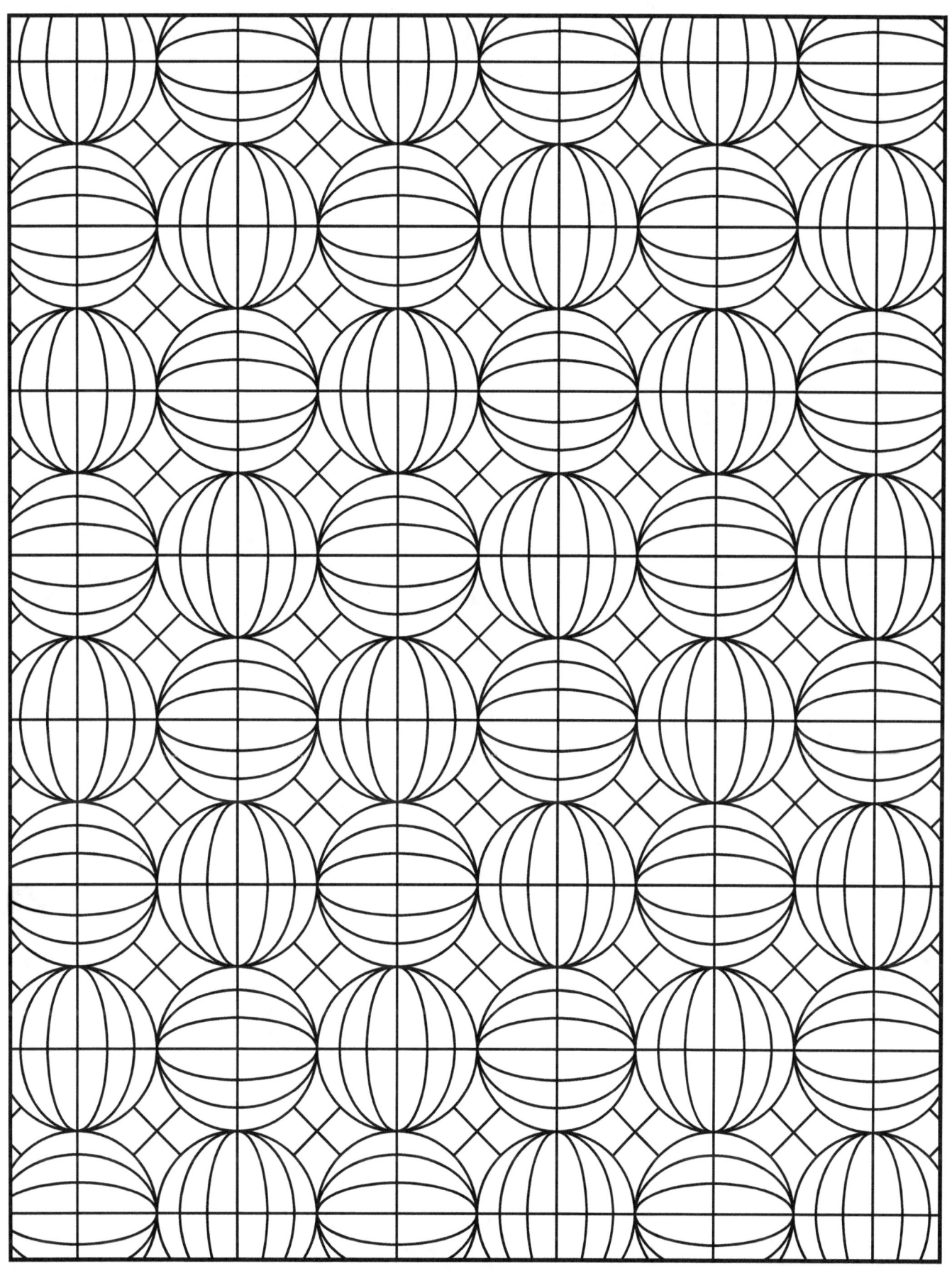

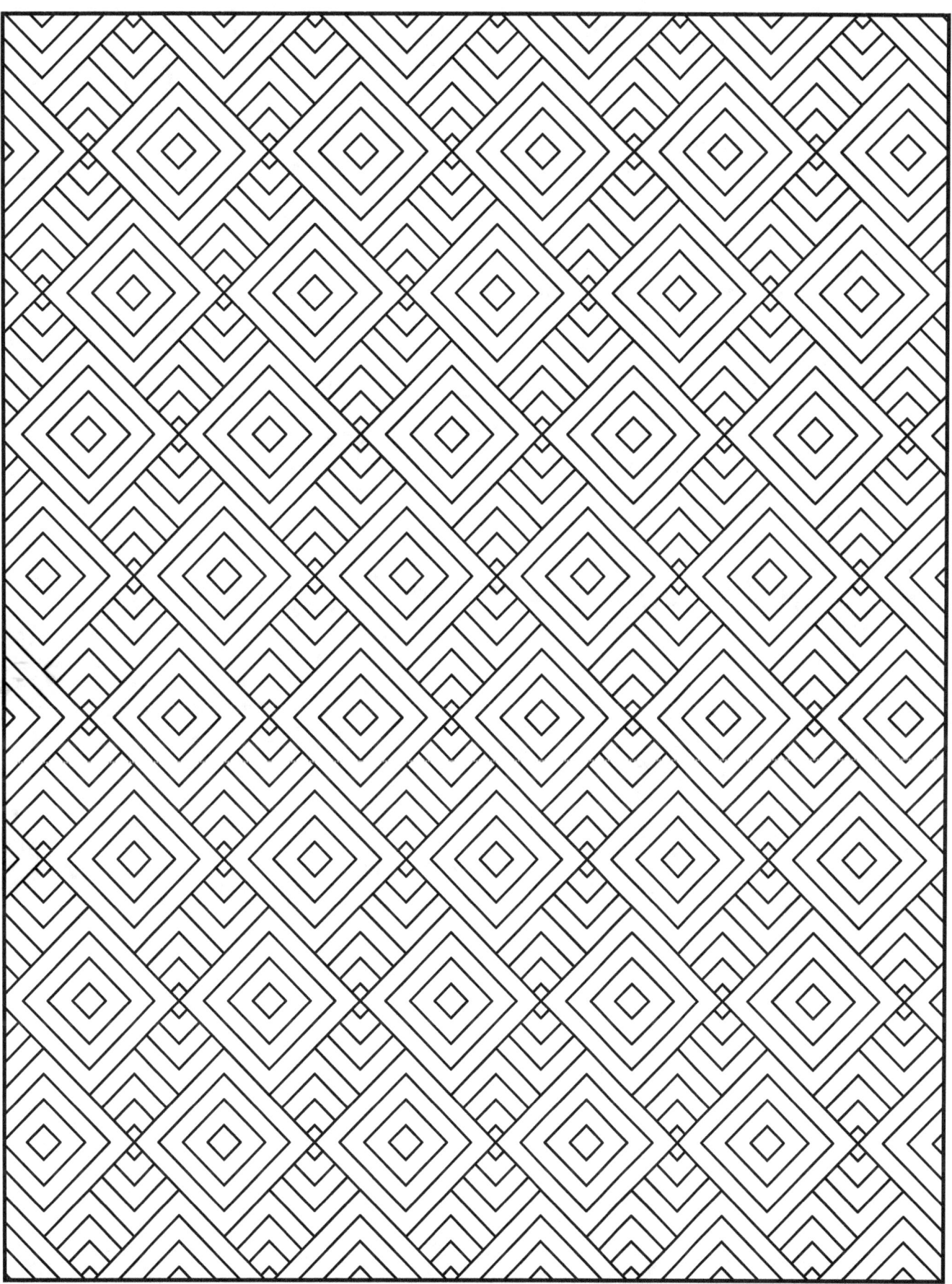

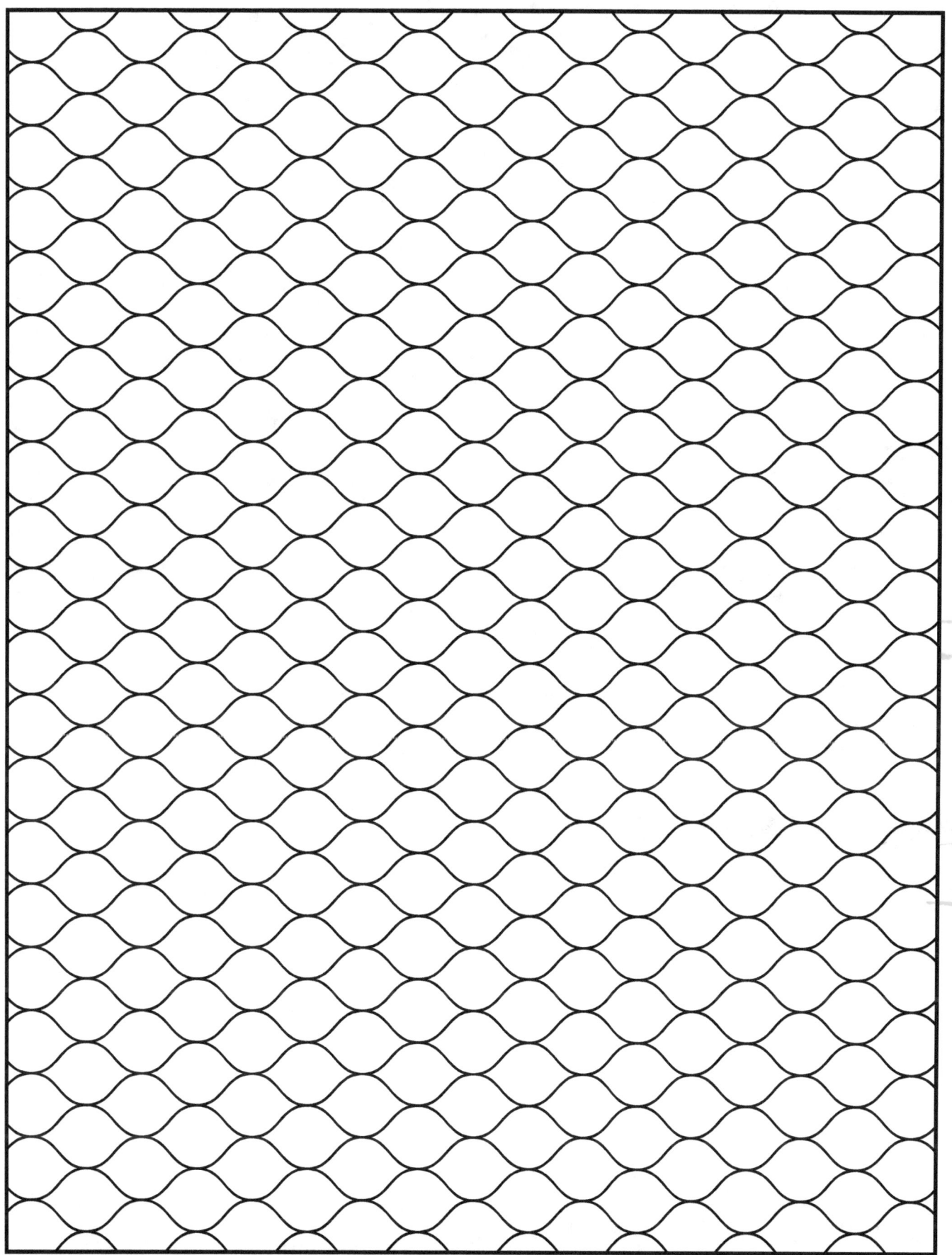

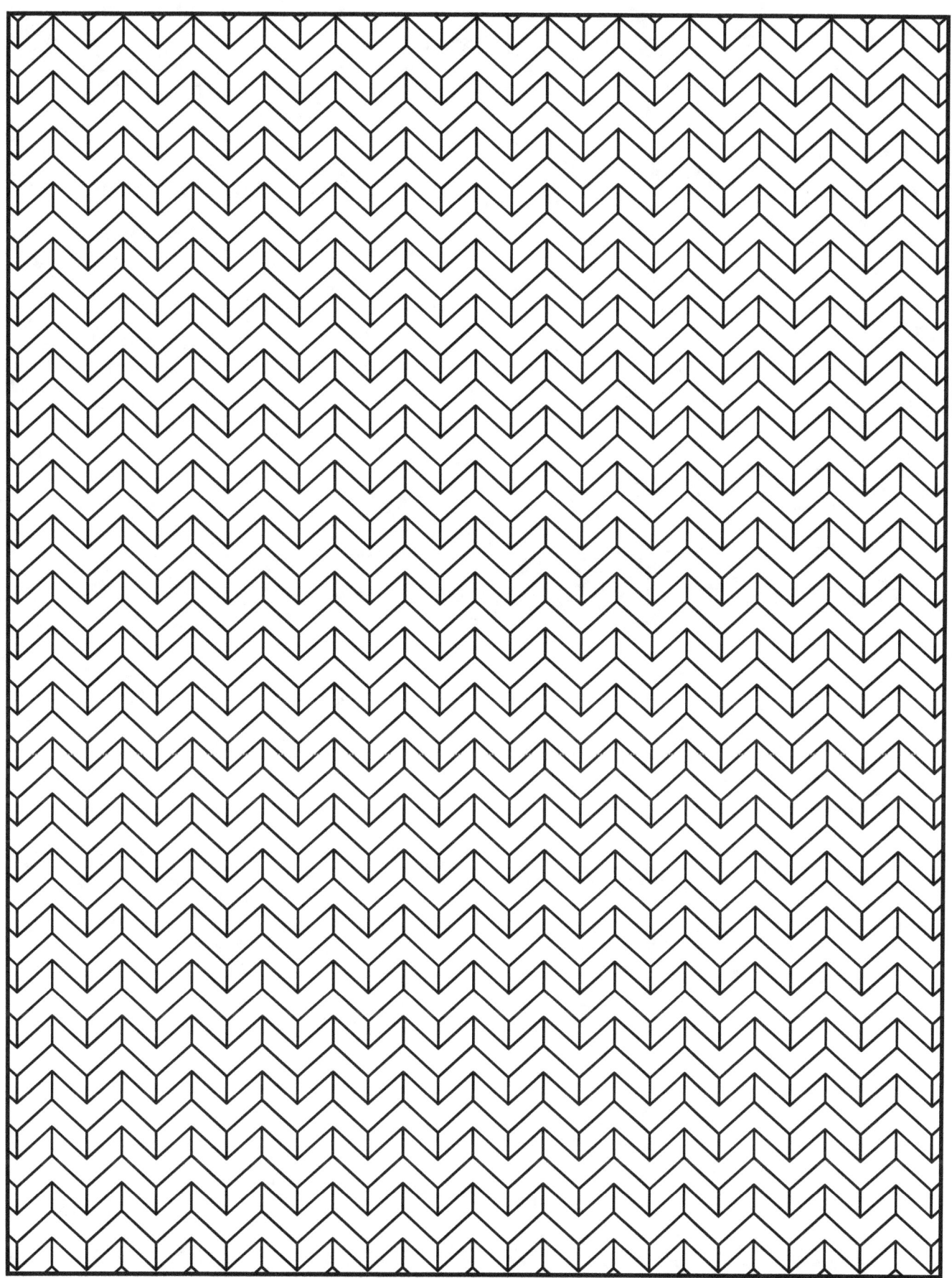

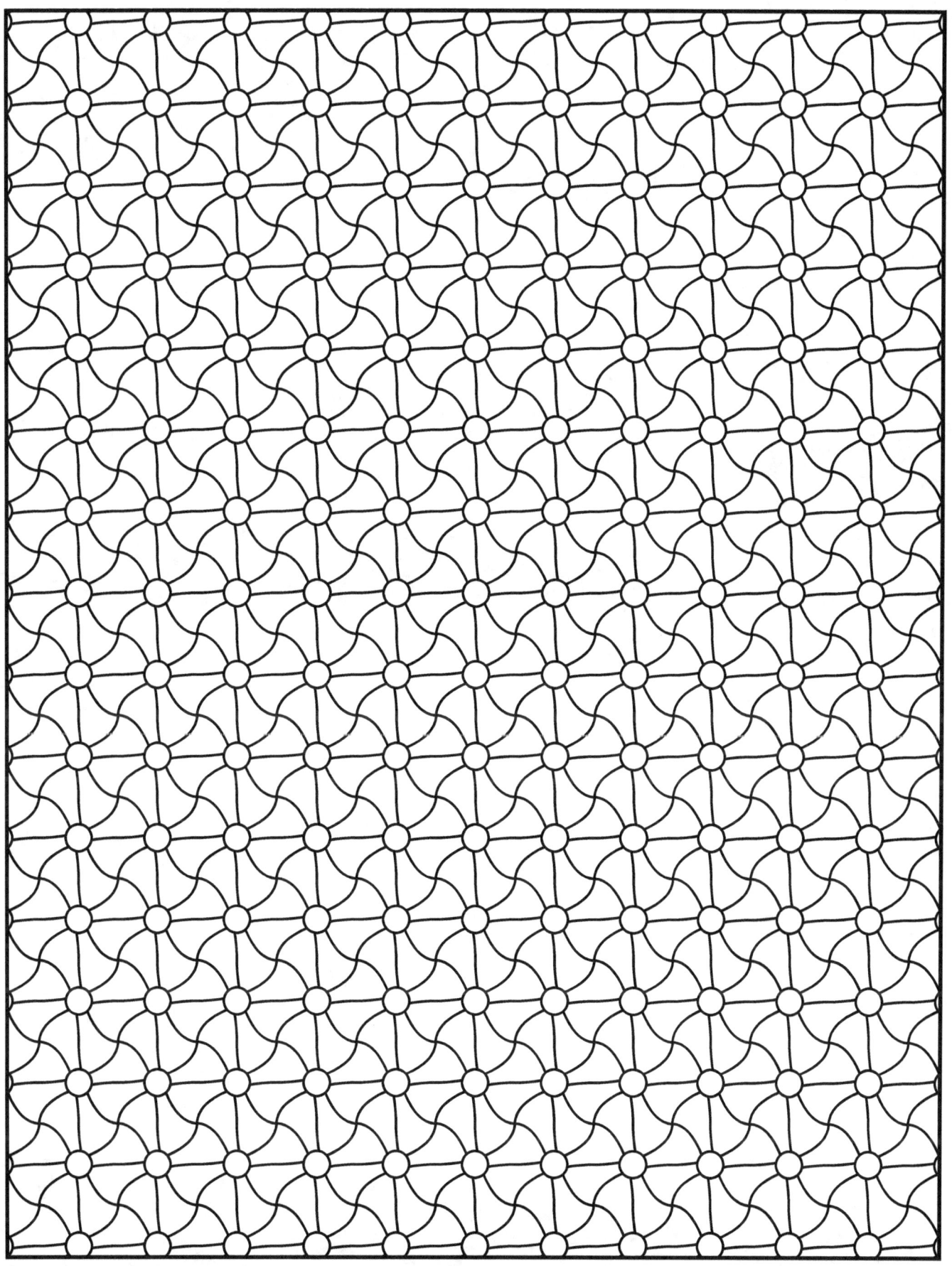

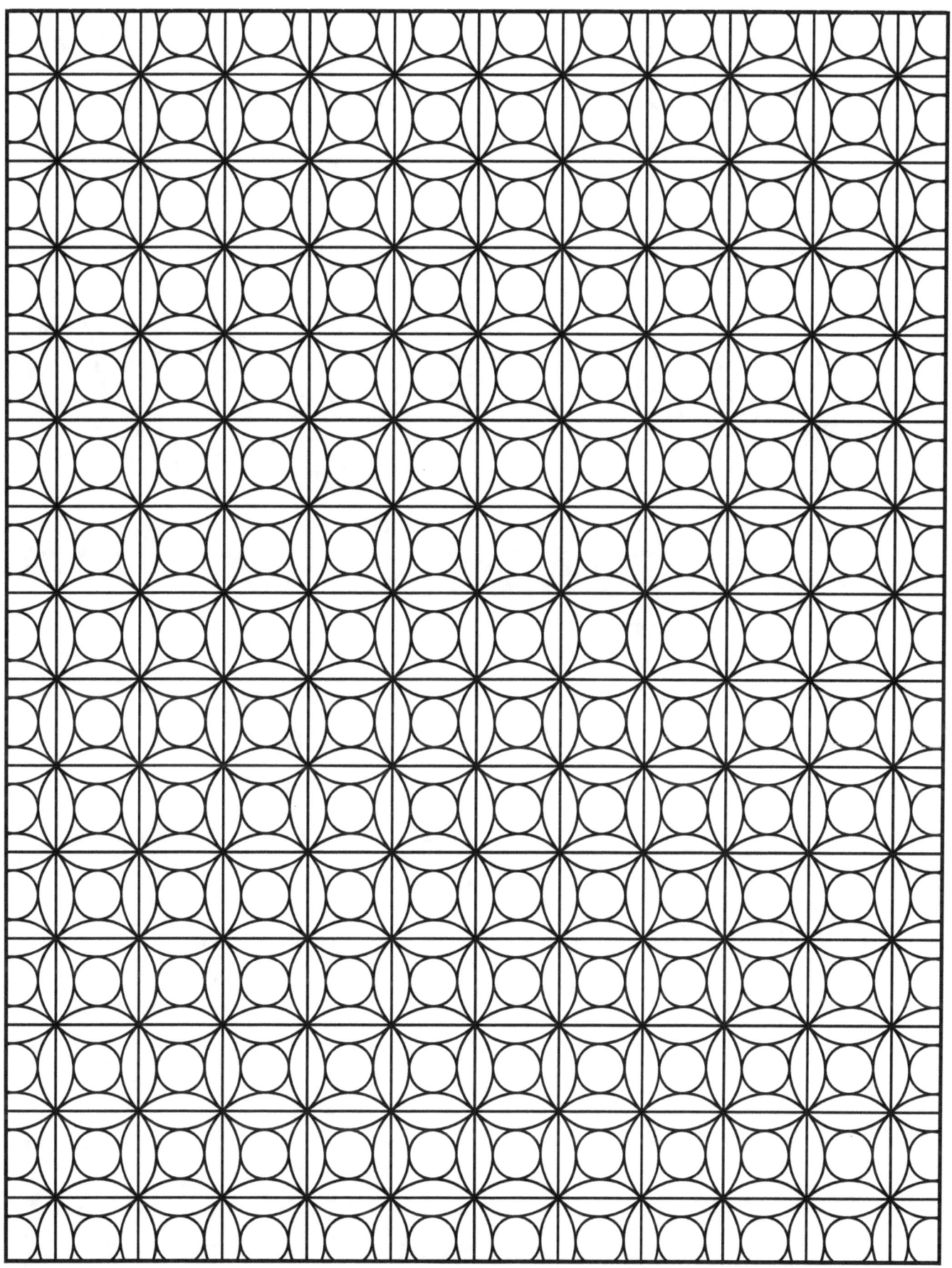

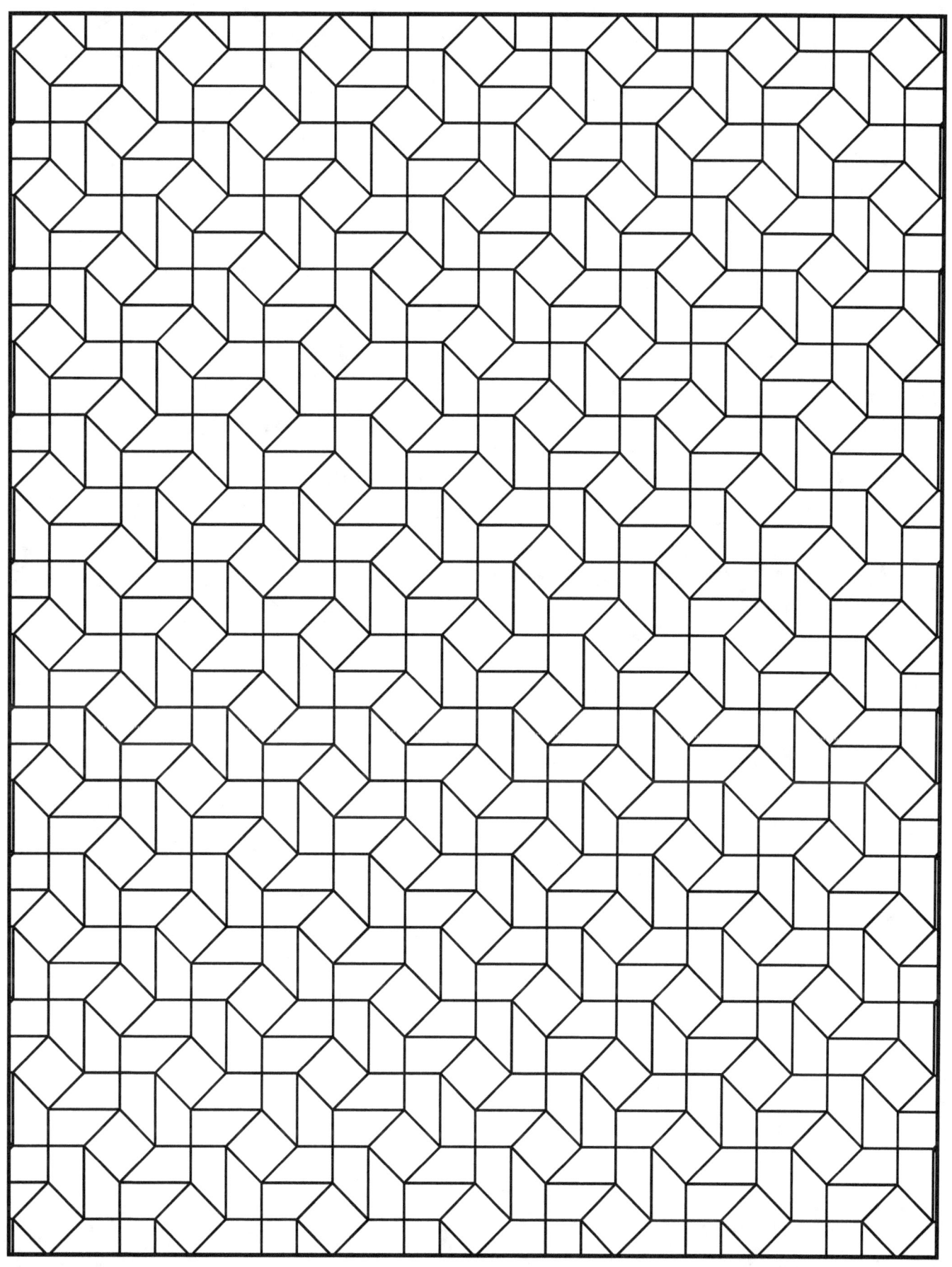

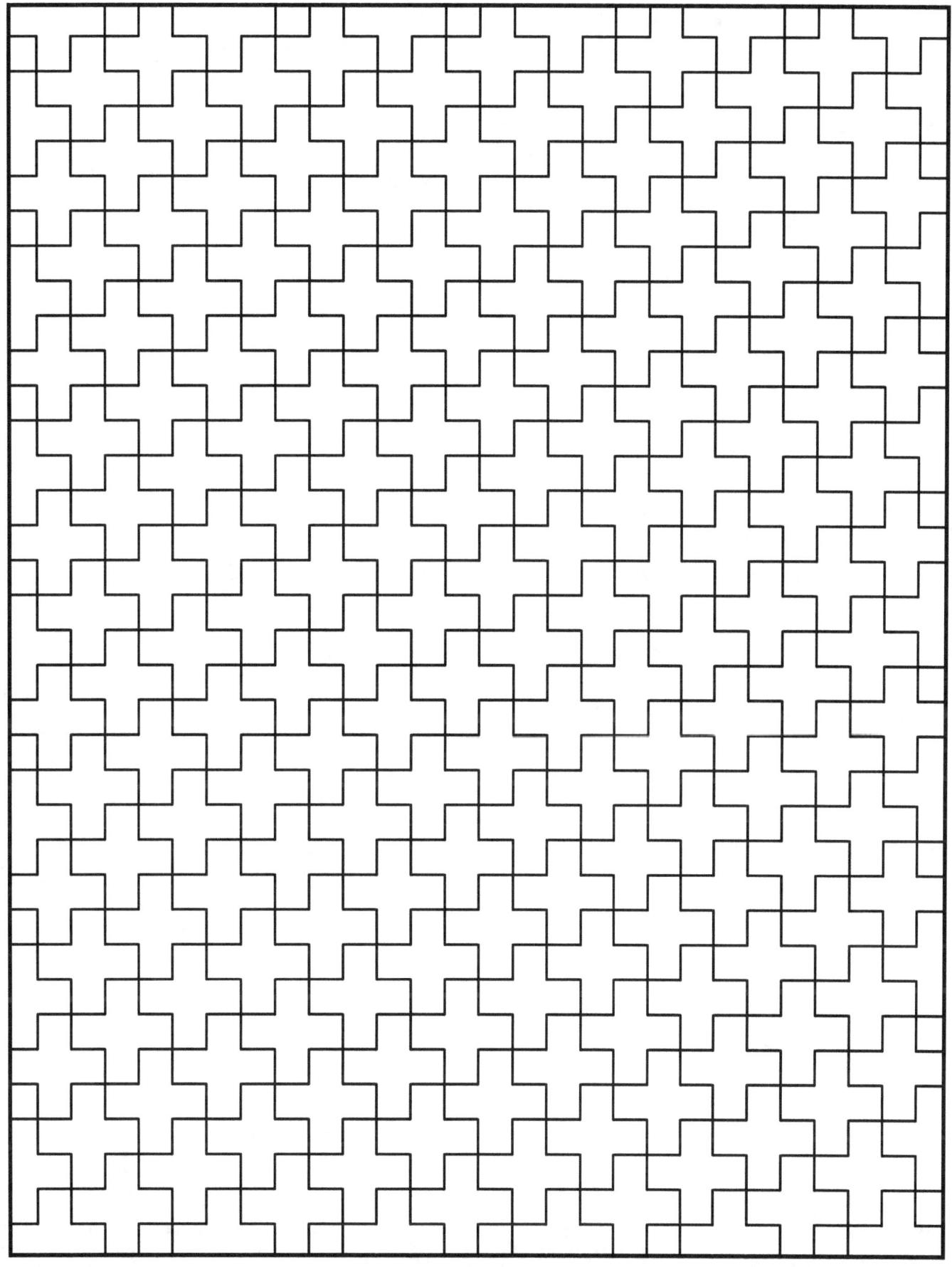

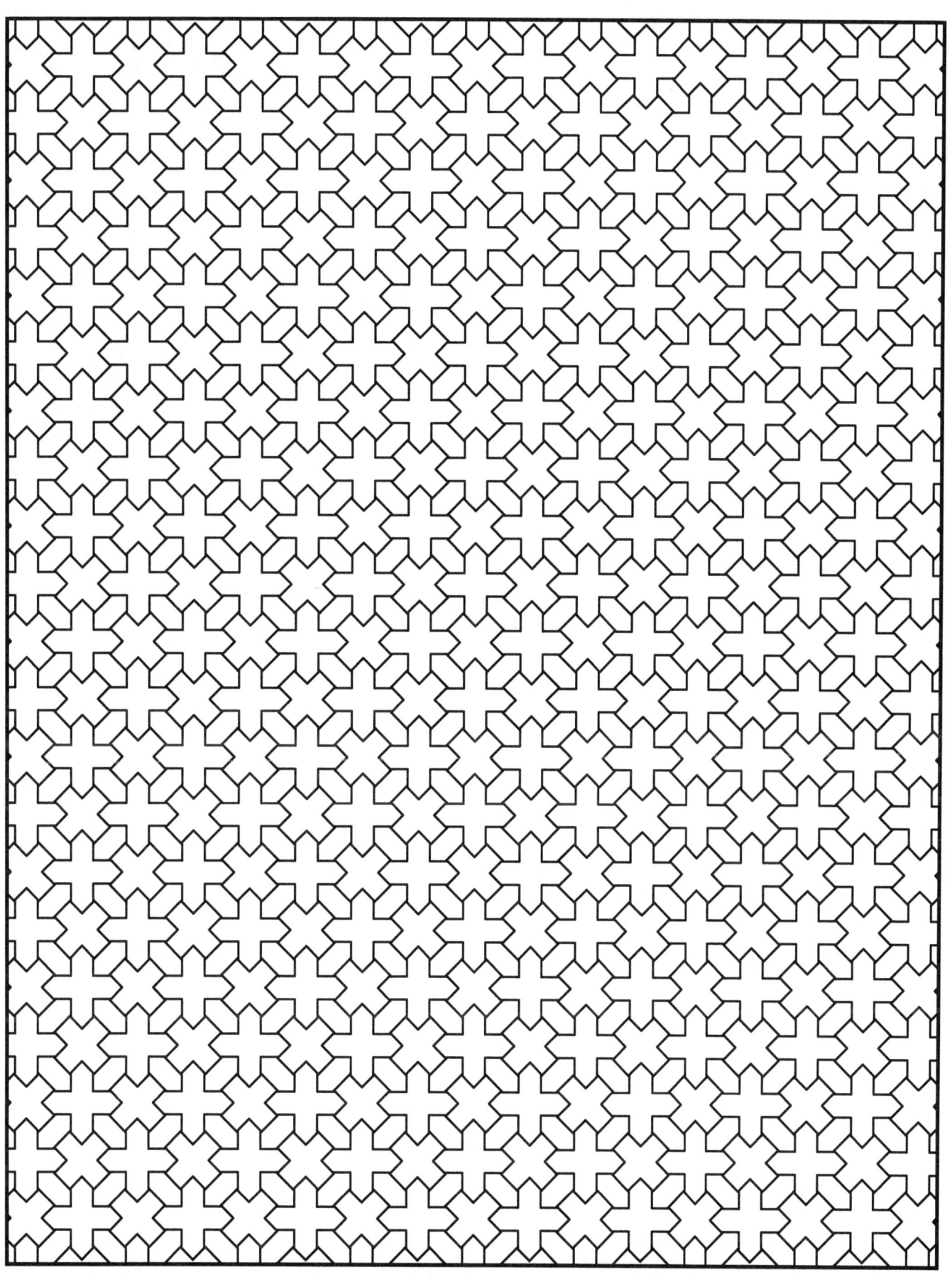

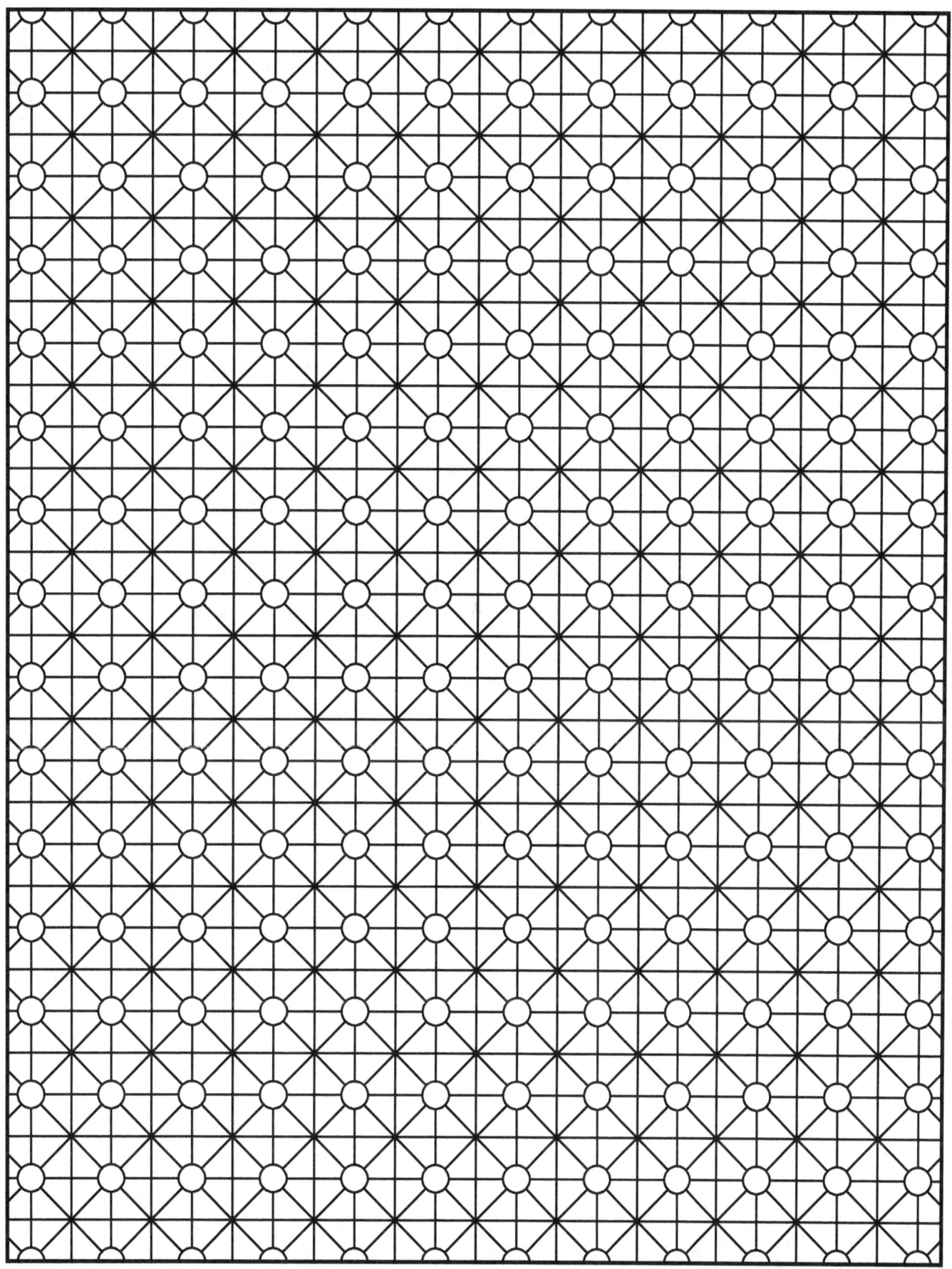

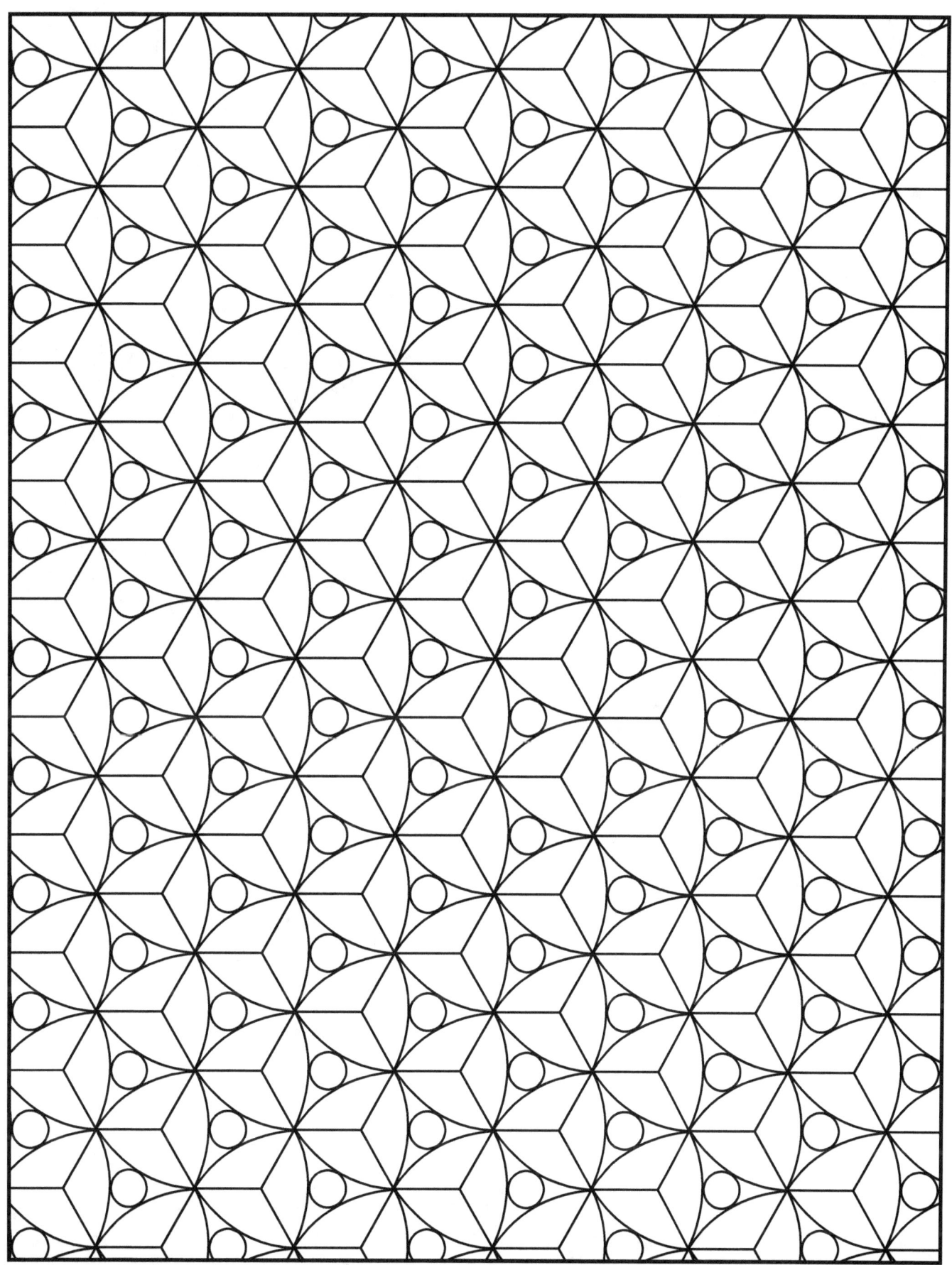

www.ingramcontent.com/pod-product-compliance
Lightning Source LLC
Chambersburg PA
CBHW081734220526

45468CB00008B/2096